Costume Doll Making

THE LAROUSSE CRAFT SERIES

Costume Doll Making

EVE McLAUGHLIN

LAROUSSE & CO. INC.
NEW YORK, N.Y.

First published in the United States by
Larousse and Co., Inc.
572 Fifth Avenue
New York, N.Y. 10036
1975

ISBN 0-88332-071-1 (hardback)
ISBN 0-88332-072-X (paperback)

Library of Congress Catalog Card No. 75-2712

Printed in Great Britain

Contents

Illustrations

Also 176 line drawings are integrated in the text.

CHAPTER 1

Background and Starting Point

Whenever archaeologists find a large-scale deposit of remains of some ancient community, they almost invariably find dolls among the pots and pans and weapons. The children had dolls, and the adults had dolls, which they called their gods, who were their confidantes and friends, to be consulted in time of trouble, and talked to for hours, in the happy knowledge that they would never criticise, or mock the owner.

Most people nowadays would think of a 'doll' either as a baby figure, with sack-like, removable garments, probably saying "Mama" and wetting its nappy, or a plastic teenage girl-doll, with a large wardrobe of clothes, and about as much personality as a cake of soap. The baby doll came in mostly when the size of normal families declined, and there was no longer a steady supply of infant brothers and sisters to dress and wet their nappies. I suspect the hand of male chauvinist manufacturers, intent on brain-washing the girl-child into a return to the nursery. The teenage doll is at least partly designed to promote the sales of fashion clothes for moppets — and who could confide in a creature which sheds its arms and legs at the slightest provocation?

The old style dolls were durable, dressed in an outfit not normally designed to be removed, and, because they were wholly or mostly hand-made, they had individuality, enhanced by years of wear and tear. Rich children's dolls were often very elaborately costumed; this was because some of them were fashion mannequins, made up by couturiers, and sent to their country customers, to show what the fashion for next season in town would be. Mama chose her styles, and then handed the sample doll over to the nursery. Poorer children had less elaborate dolls, sometimes made in the winter evenings by their parents, who would share the labour of carving a wooden puppet, and dressing it in the local costume, or in the garb of some trade or occupation. Where these old dolls survive, they are valuable family heirlooms, in a way factory-made products can never be. There is nothing personal about a doll that every girl in the street has, and even in remote country districts, where there is a recognisable national or regional costume, the whole thing has become commercialised, and crudely dressed, plastic-bodied, baby dolls are churned out to satisfy the tourist trade. The pop-eyed, pot-bellied doll, with painted-on socks and button shoes, with a bit of tartan cloth stuck round it, is an insult to Scottish soldiers.

Fortunately, more and more people are getting interested in filling the gap. With a little know-how, and some practice, anyone can create a doll that is hand-made, individual in design and style, and a source of pleasure and pride to maker and family alike. The deep satisfaction of creating something which lasts, in this world of disposables, is worth the time that the making takes. It can also become a family project, involving the boys as well as the girls, for other skills are needed besides sewing. Help with shaping wire mounts and stiffeners, carving or modelling faces, and making little accessories to complete the doll is always welcome.

Costume dolls can be made as big or small, stylised or detailed, glamorous or rough-ethnic, as you wish. If you are a complete beginner, it is easiest to start with a simple, fairly large doll, dressed in a basic style which is representative of a country or period, rather than a detailed copy of, say, the marriage costume of a burgher's daughter in Unter Schloppenburg in 1797. The simpler doll enables you to get the hang of working on a small scale, and gives you the chance to exploit any particular talents you may have. If you can embroider, or have always wanted to, now is the time to experiment, with about 3 in of decoration around a bodice. Try out your ability in face designing, and hair styling, and practise the techniques you will need later, when making more complicated dolls.

It may seem that it would be easier to begin with a little doll, but, believe me, it is not. People's fingers do not shrink to match the size of the model, and tackling a mini-doll when you seem to have a collection of ten enormous thumbs is one way to put you off doll work for life. Besides, until you have a fair collection of dolls to show, there is a lot to be said for making something big enough not to be sat on by a hefty son who just hasn't noticed your tiny effort at creativity. Once you have mastered the art, then there is great use for small costume dolls, as part of a large landscape or scene, in which the whole family or school class can take a hand.

More complicated dolls can represent a particular historical period, or the style worn in a precise village, or by a person in a special occupation or position. The more detailed and realistic you wish the result to be, the more important it is to have good illustrations from which to work. Line drawings and coloured photographs are easier to work from than black and white ones. Travel posters, holiday brochures, and children's story books are good as sources for simple national costumes, and the tourist bureaux of various

countries often have packs of literature with illustrations of elaborate costumes from definite districts. Museums often have models of historical costumes, and although they are touchy about visitors taking photographs, they may have postcards for sale, or rough sketches can be made, with notes on the kind of material used. Don't forget the back views as well, for some costumes have very elaborate arrangements there.

There are very many books about historical costumes, some of which are listed in the Appendix. From these, you can learn how the different styles of garment were constructed, and make a model with all the period detail correct. A step further is to make a portrait doll, of a historical person, with a carefully modelled face, and clothes of the right period. There are usually paintings of these persons, in at least half length, so you can reproduce the actual clothes they wore as shown, and fill in the unseen parts from other pictures showing what was worn with that style of dress or doublet, etc. Art galleries, and books of paintings will furnish you with models to work from.

Television series set in earlier times usually have the characters' costumes very thoroughly researched, and if they are on the screen long enough, it is possible to make a sketch of particular outfits from all angles. The cinema is not so good as a source of information, because of the difficulty of arranging light to draw by, but a person with good visual memory might recall enough. Sometimes there are exhibitions of costumes used in a play or film, and reproductions of the designs may be available from the television or film company. Costumes are usually made up in paler colours than would have been used, because of the deficiencies of colour transmission, and this can be corrected by using deeper and brighter shades in dressing the doll.

An interesting set of models can be made of people in various occupations. Soldiers, sailors and airmen are popular, but need to be very carefully made, if some ancient gentleman is not to go red in the face because the headgear is at the wrong angle, or the boots insufficiently shiny. Illustrations are readily available, in encyclopaedias, children's books, military or naval histories, and give-away cards with foodstuffs, etc. Wall-charts of uniforms are sold to schools, through educational publishers, and, if a particular regiment's uniform of a special date is required, the regimental historian will usually be happy to assist.

Civilians with a recognisable 'uniform' for their jobs include fishermen, doctors, policemen, pirates, gipsies, old-time farm labourers, and ballet dancers. Some of these will be best shown on 'character' dolls, where the face and possibly body is more or less grotesque or caricatured. This also applies to the fantasy dolls, representing witches, devils, goblins, and the other creatures that children love to be scared by.

CHAPTER 2

Making the Body

Making a doll figure for dressing is perhaps the most difficult, and most important, part of the operation. The most elegant clothes will never look good on a saggy, baggy rag bundle with a droopy neck. It is perfectly possible to buy a factory-made doll for dressing, or sometimes to acquire an old doll whose clothes need replacing. A finely modelled head in china of an antique doll is a great thing to have, even when the cloth body has decayed, and deserves the best efforts to rehabilitate it.

The modern plastic doll is not so good. Baby dolls, and some little girl dolls, are made with infantile faces, and bottom-heavy figures. Teenage dolls are easy to find, but tend to have modern styled hair, made-up faces and, too often, a curious monkey look about the lower jaw. The hair can sometimes be changed, and the heavy eye make-up carefully wiped off with either acetone (nail varnish remover) or dry cleaning fluid. Use these in a well ventilated place, and mop away the eye paint with a tiny tissue, so that it does not spread down the cheek.

If you can find a suitable doll, this may be a painless way of starting a collection. Most doll makers, however, eventually like to have a go at making bodies, because then the doll is absolutely individual, and no one can copy it exactly, even beginning with the same pattern. Also, the basic body shape changed with the centuries, mainly because the undergarments or corsets altered, forcing the pliant flesh into whatever shape was fashionable at the time. This is achieved in doll-making by cutting and stuffing the doll body to the right shape before the clothes are put on. Different methods of head and body construction give different degrees of realism, and the doll maker can decide at the outset the kind of effect required, and chose a body accordingly.

Dolls can be constructed using a very simple framework of wire and corks, cardboard, plastic bottles, rough wood or any household and garden oddments. I have given a number of suggestions for framework dolls in Chapter Nine. These are most suitable for small-scale work, particularly for inclusion in landscapes and scenes, made by the whole class or family, where the dolls are usually fixed firmly in position. Larger dolls, especially those in the more elaborate costumes, get picked up and studied at close quarters, and most of those who inspect will turn the doll upside down, and look at the actual body. It is galling, to say the least, to have all the elegant upper dressing ignored, in favour of a comment like "Oh, so you used a Gloppo bottle. It leaves my hair all frizzy." It is worth being thorough, even if a body with legs instead of a solid base is more difficult to mount when finished.

MATERIALS FOR MAKING THE BODY

The body needs to be as stiff and self supporting as possible when finished, but it should have some flexibility, to ease the dressing, and posing the finished figure. This is mostly achieved by inserting wire in the trunk and limbs, and using strong cloth, so that the figure can be tightly stuffed.

The kind of wire to be used should be one that the individual worker can handle comfortably. It is no use choosing something so stiff that it takes six strong men to bend it, or even cut it, because strong men are rarely there when you settle to a session of doll making. The kind of flexible wire used in the garden for tying up plants is ideal, easy to cut and bend, but firm when put in position. It can always be doubled for strength. A useful type of wire is sold very cheaply in 1,000-yard rolls as ex-Army signal wire. This is covered in plastic, and quite pleasant to handle. I have given directions for using this kind of wire, but anything available can be used.

Bodies come under a lot of strain when they are turned and stuffed, so the cloth should be strong and firm, and the stitching done by machine if possible, or closely done. For general purposes, old sheets can be used, discarding any weak sections, and either pre-dyed or painted and coloured later. The skin should be a light pinky-beige, for European races, and paler for delicate ladies than for rugged peasants. If commercial dye is not available, something of the right effect can be obtained with cochineal and cold tea, cautiously used for soaking. It is better to err on the side of lightness, and paint on later, than to end up trying to dress a raspberry ice on legs. Poster paints, or felt-tip pens will produce features which look quite good. Try drawing the features and using colours on paper, and on a piece of the body cloth before applying to the actual face.

Special Materials for Skin

For special purposes, a top skin for the face can be made of stockinet, satin, nylon stockings, or kid or chamois leather. The stockinet is not the thin sort sold for cleaning rags, but the thicker, closer weave, such as old ladies' petticoats were made of before Granny discovered nylon. This may be found in a few old-fashioned drapers/dry goods stores, or craft shops, or Auntie Maggie might be persuaded to trade in her old undies for something glamorous in a synthetic material. Stockinet, and nylon tights, are softer and more flexible than sheeting, so care must be

taken not to get a distorted effect. It may be necessary to line them with a thicker fabric, and just add a thin layer of stuffing, to make nose and chin, under the stockinet.

Society ladies, especially in the eighteenth century, displayed large amounts of upper torso, and the basic body can be given an extra layer of satin, with concealed seams, where necessary, on face and shoulders. Satin looks fine, but it should not be put under strain at the stitches, or they will cut into the fabric like a wound. Some synthetics, if you can find the right pink colour, will pass as skin, but care must be taken to hem the edge firmly without producing a lump. Ladies with hard edges and ladies with runs in their bosoms are not the best quality!

Antique dolls often had 'skin' of kid leather. This looks elegant, and will even mould into features, if wetted in small areas and handled very carefully, but it needs delicate handling, and neat stitching with a thin but sharp needle. It is expensive to buy, but enough may be found in an old, split-fingered glove for covering the head and shoulders. Some grades of chamois leather are useful, though some is too thick and some so thin it bulges out of shape.

Stuffing

The doll body can be stuffed with almost any soft, mouldable material. The traditional stuffing is either sawdust, horsehair or kapok. Sawdust must be absolutely bone-dry, and fine, from a bench saw rather than a handsaw, and must be rammed down very hard; it tends, therefore, to be inflexible for dressing. Horsehair must be sterilised, and is not readily come by, although anyone with a stable or a decaying Victorian sofa might like to try it. Kapok is super-soft, and packs down into a beautifully smooth, even filling, but it is so light that it flies around, and the room gets covered with a very fine fall-out. If you use it, work on a newspaper or old sheet, wear an apron, and don't try to drink coffee at the same time. It does give the best results, and is obtainable from craft shops, some furniture stores and also where material for cushion covers is sold.

Cotton-wool, in the grades used for cleansing purposes, is much cheaper than kapok, and stays out of your hair and mouth, but, even if it is pulled into small pieces, it has not quite as smooth a finish as kapok, unless great care is taken to smooth out the lumps. A mixture of the two, with kapok filling in the tiny hollows, is ideal.

Polyurethane foam can be bought cheaply in small scraps, but I do not recommend its use. It is incurably lumpy, and will not pack down to a firm filling. There is also a danger of fire, since, if it becomes hot — as it might on a mantelshelf or table near the fire — it gives off inflammable gases, which readily ignite, and can cause a nasty fire.

Old sweaters, and other clothes which have reached the ragbag can be shredded up very small, and used to stuff dolls, though they may be lumpy, unless the rags are well pushed down. They, and any recovered stuffing out of old cushions and pillows, will do very well though, to eke out if you are short of finer fillings, and they do give you the satisfaction of using up what would otherwise be wasted.

BEWARE BABIES!   If the finished doll is to live in a household with very small children, then safety precautions must be taken. Wire stiffening and any sharp trimmings, and lead-based paint, too, should be avoided. The most docile little angel will chew and tug at the doll until the wire pokes out, then aim it at the darling next door. The only stiffening to be used in the circumstances is a piece of $\frac{1}{2}$ in dowelling wood, or thick solid plastic rod, so it cannot snap. All cloth and stitching needs to be super-strong, to leave no gaps for tiny fingers — and, just in case, the stuffing should be kapok or cotton-wool, which seems to be non-poisonous when eaten.

MAKING THE BODY
Method One
The simplest type of body is a rag doll, with body and head cut in one. The kind with least work in the making is *Flat Fanny*, which has two identical sides, and simply stitches together as indicated in Figure 1. The big snag about this doll is that the face is very flat, and can only have caricature features sewn or drawn on it. However, this is a popular style of commercial doll at the moment, since manufacturers have also discovered how quickly and simply it can be made, with very little labour cost. These dolls are generally badly finished, and if you want to make your own, then you cannot fail to improve on the shop article.

To do this, use the body pattern for *Rag Rosy* (Figure 3) substituting the head pattern with the *Flat Fanny* head — Figure 2. Trace the body and neck of *Rag Rosy*, and the head of *Fanny*, and stick the two together, superimposing the neck lines. Cut out two identical pieces and make up as for *Rag Rosy*, except for the shaping of the head.

Rag Rosy herself is also made in two identical pieces, back and front, but her head is cut larger, and shaped by darts to form a ball. Her pattern, complete, is shown in Figure 3. Trace it on strong paper to make a pattern for repeated use.

Cut out the body shape twice, in strong material, and, with the wrong side of the material facing you, stitch together the darts, on the dotted lines. The head sections will now look like two halves of a tennis ball. Place right sides together, and stitch all the way round twice, on the edge and $\frac{1}{4}$ in inside this, leaving gaps at A -B and C- D in the side and head to aid turning and stuffing. Clip the outer line of stitches on the curves, and turn the body inside out, using a blunt pencil or stick to push the limbs into place, taking care not to make a hole.

Stuff the legs and arms, ramming the kapok or other stuffing well down into the toes and hands, since it is difficult to ease it along afterwards, and loose stuffing makes a flabby doll. Next pad the bottom of the body, and insert the length of dowel or plastic rod through the head. Continue stuffing the body and head, shaping the curves for the upper torso with extra stuffing as you go. Turn in the raw edges, and oversew the gaps into place, firmly. The head will have a certain amount of chin shape, and stuffing can be rolled to make a nose projection.

The heads for both *Fanny* and *Rosy* can be given features afterwards. *Fanny* can be embroidered, appliquéd or drawn, with paints or felt-tip pens. As her face is quite flat, the features should be kept very simple, and tend to caricature. Study children's cartoons and comics for ideas. *Rosy* can be embroidered or appliquéd, but looks best painted in poster colours or drawn with felt-pens. Her features should be simple, but need not be caricatured. Experiment, on paper first, with the type of decoration, till you find what you can do best.

Method Two

More elaborate dolls look better on more complicated bodies, which are wired and articulated, so that the finished doll can be posed to display the costume to best advantage. There are two basic patterns, which can be varied for individual dolls.

CLOTH CHARLOTTE (Figures 4–6) is the basic female figure, and can very easily have the bust and hip measurements adjusted, by an even increase all round, for a more matronly figure, or a decrease for a boyish, or young girl, shape. If the waist is much decreased, it will be easier to divide the pattern at the waist, to ease turning, and oversew the parts together on the right side. Don't increase the waist much, since older ladies wore tight corsets, and more layers of clothes.

CLOTH CHARLES (Figures 7–9) is the basic young male, who is taller, broader-shouldered and not so curvy in the waist. He can be increased to make an older male figure, by adding to the waist and hips, more than to the shoulders. Special effects, for grotesque dolls, can be achieved by variations on these two patterns, or by padding on top of the finished torso, although a great deal can be managed by bending the wires, and selective stuffing of the basic shapes.

The arms and legs should be matched to the body and increased if you increase the trunk size. They are cut as oblongs, stitched into cylinders for strength, then shaped with the second row of stitching, all on the wrong side (see page 19). Clip the curves at knee and elbow, and turn the limbs inside out, using a pencil or rod to push the ends into shape. Start with the legs, and stuff a little padding into the toe. Cut a wire twice as long as the leg, plus 2 in, and twist the cut ends together (Figure 10 a). Fold the wire in half, with the cut ends half-way down the leg, and small loops at either end. If you are using thick wire, then a single thickness down the leg, with loops at tops and bottom, can be used (Figure 10 b). Stuff the leg, keeping the wire in the centre as you work, and taking care to ram the kapok etc. well down, but avoiding unsightly lumps which spoil the line of the leg. When the stuffing reaches within $\frac{1}{2}$ in of the top, snip a tiny slit where the wire loop touches the cloth, turn in the raw edges, and oversew them together under the loop. You should now have a firm leg, with a half loop of wire projecting like a basket handle at the top (Figure 11). Repeat the process for the other leg and the two arms.

You will notice that there are no shaped fingers, and no projecting feet. A hand cannot be made so small in a realistic way, so it is best to indicate the slope of the fingers on top of the stuffed hand if you wish. In cases where a really shaped hand is needed for some particularly elegant effect, it may be necessary to use a plastic or china moulded hand from a manufactured doll, or to cast a hand in plaster and mould it in one of the materials suggested, for heads, in Chapter Three.

Similarly, feet cut from cloth in the correct size for the figure could never be strong enough to support the doll. A better method is to stiffen and stuff the toe of the shoe or boot, and attach it to the leg as a finished article. This eliminates a weak point in the

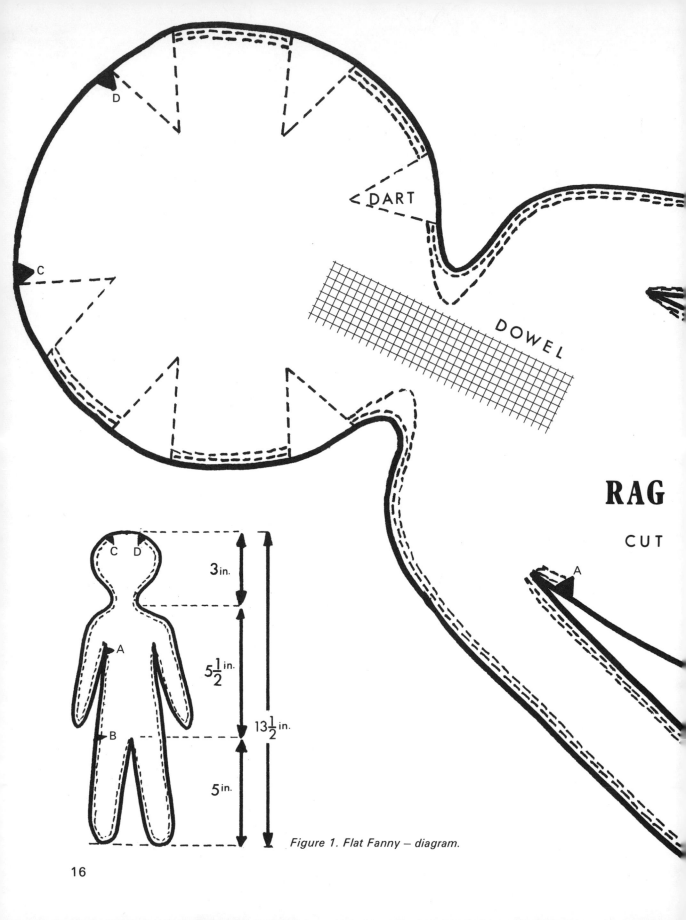

DART

DOWEL

RAG

CUT

A

C D

3 in.

5½ in.

13½ in.

5 in.

A

B

Figure 1. Flat Fanny — diagram.

16

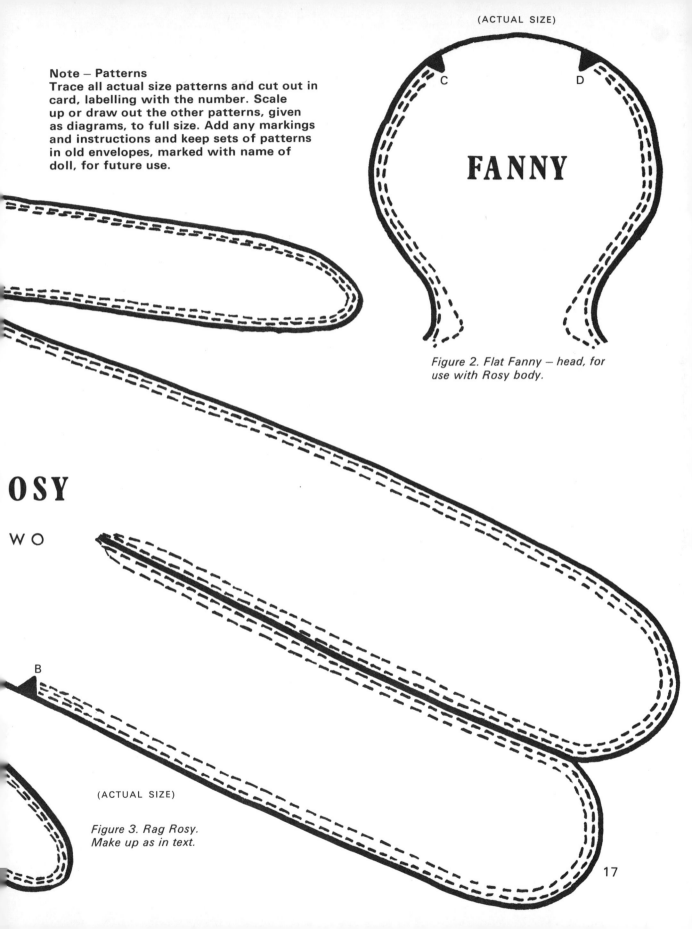

Note – Patterns
Trace all actual size patterns and cut out in card, labelling with the number. Scale up or draw out the other patterns, given as diagrams, to full size. Add any markings and instructions and keep sets of patterns in old envelopes, marked with name of doll, for future use.

FANNY

Figure 2. Flat Fanny — head, for use with Rosy body.

OSY

WO

B

(ACTUAL SIZE)

*Figure 3. Rag Rosy.
Make up as in text.*

17

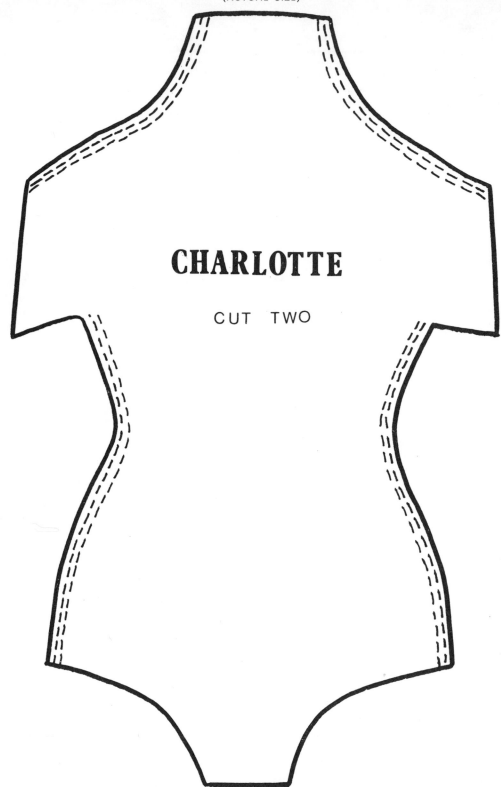

CHARLOTTE

CUT TWO

Figure 4. Cloth Charlotte.
Make up as in text.

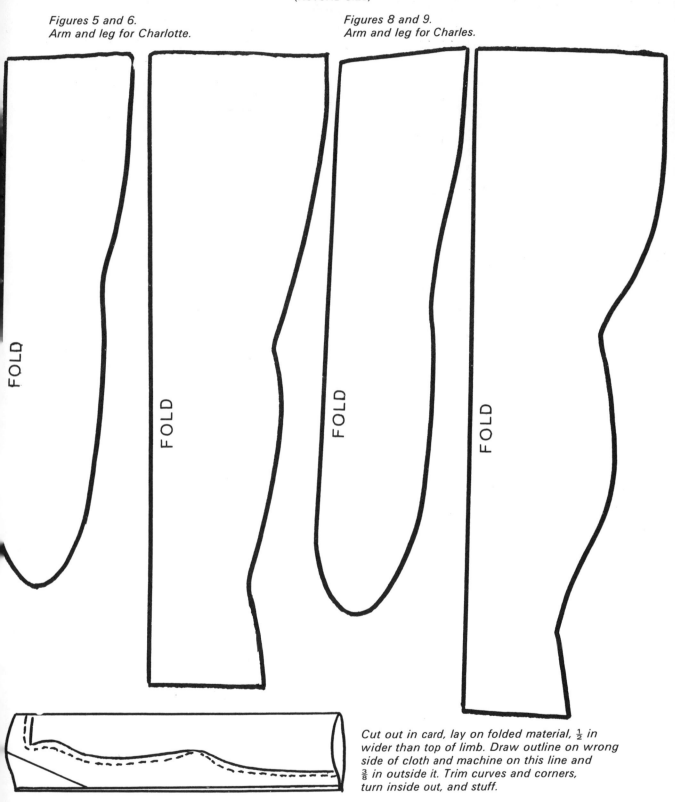

Figures 5 and 6.
Arm and leg for Charlotte.

Figures 8 and 9.
Arm and leg for Charles.

FOLD

FOLD

FOLD

FOLD

Cut out in card, lay on folded material, $\frac{1}{2}$ in wider than top of limb. Draw outline on wrong side of cloth and machine on this line and $\frac{3}{8}$ in outside it. Trim curves and corners, turn inside out, and stuff.

CHARLES

CUT TWO

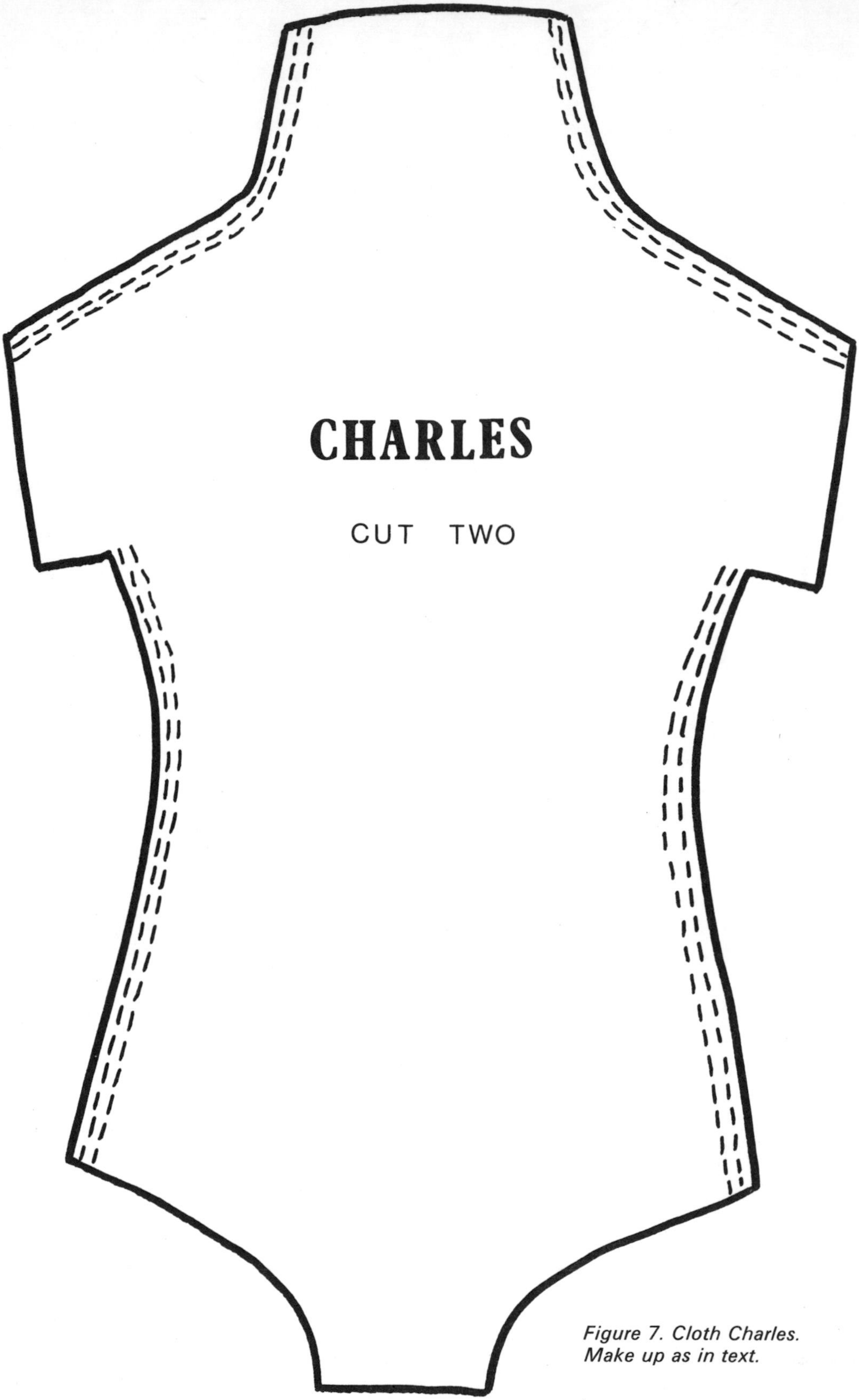

Figure 7. Cloth Charles.
Make up as in text.

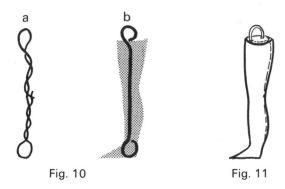

a   b

Fig. 10   Fig. 11

Figure 10. Leg (a) Thin wire stiffening, twisted. (b) Thicker wire.
Figure 11. Leg, completely stuffed, with wire loop.

making of a doll's leg, and enables more variation in the attachment of the footgear to the mount on which you display the finished doll. This is often something which you will not want to decide until you have made most of the doll, and can see how well it will balance.

When the limbs are ready, make up the trunk by stitching the two pieces of the pattern together, right sides facing. Leave the neck, base and the underarm open, but machine the rest on the edge and $\frac{1}{4}$ in inside this line. Clip curves, and turn the trunk to the right side. Baste under all raw edges, using the smallest possible turning. You will now have something that resembles a skinny, old-fashioned swim suit, but this is deliberate. By the time it has layers of costume on top, a 'normal' waist would look like a slimming ad — Before.

Cut a piece of wire twice as long as the trunk, plus 4 in. Thread an end as long as the trunk through one leg loop, twist the other end round it, then across through the other leg loop, leaving a 'pelvis' length between the two legs. Twist the two free ends of the wire around each other a few times to make a 'spine', and leave the free ends pointing straight up for a while (Figure 12). Slide the 'swim-suit' over the legs and pull it up until the upper leg is just covered by the suit edge on the outer side ('hip'). Oversew neatly into position, then pad out the crotch section,

and stitch this firmly into place, overlapping the edges. Then stuff the lower half of the body, easing the framework of the 'pelvis' a little upwards as you go, and padding well around it, until the lower part of the body is firm and smooth, with no sag around the tops of the legs.

Next, insert the free ends of the wire through the arm loops, and place the arms in position, pulling the ends of the wires out through the neck gap, and twisting them roughly into place (Figure 13). Complete the stuffing of the upper body, through the neck and underarm gaps, twisting the wire more precisely as you go. Stitch the arms firmly into place by sewing down the shoulders of the trunk, as invisibly as possible. They will have enough flexibility to be set in a pose, but not to swing floppily beside the body.

This completes the stuffing of the body, and the head can now be attached. The precise method of doing this depends on the kind of head that you are using (for which see the next chapter). If it is a cloth head, stiffened by a neck rod, then push the rod

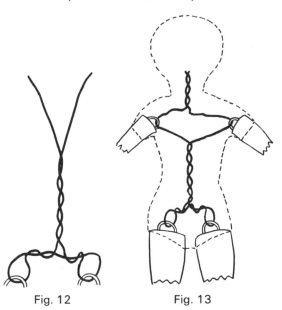

Fig. 12   Fig. 13

Figure 12. Body wire. Pelvis and leg loops. Keep wire central while stuffing.
Figure 13. Body wire. Complete layout of wiring for tunk, with loose ends for attachment to head wire.

firmly down into the body stuffing, twisting the top wire around it as you work, and stitch tightly round the neckline. If it is a solid moulded head, it should have a projecting loop of wire, which is hooked on to the body wire, and the cloth neck of the trunk is then gathered slightly, and stitched tightly round it. If you feel there is any risk of drooping, add wire stiffening to correct this.

Child dolls, to make a family group, can be adapted from the *Charlotte* pattern or the *Rosy* pattern, scaled down in height and leg length, as well as width. The heads are disproportionately large, however, and the features placed lower down the face. A commercial little girl doll will show you what lines to follow here. Really small dolls, for doll's house work, can also be scaled down from the *Charlotte* body (but see Chapter Nine, 'Little People').

CHAPTER 3

Heads and Faces

The darted ball head, used for *Rosy*, is good enough for normal purposes, but if the work you are putting into the costume is very complicated, you will probably feel that the face should be more precise, too. For making portraits of historical persons, you will certainly need a mask, attached to a roughly shaped ball head (Figure 14) or a fully moulded whole head.

THE PROFILE HEAD

The simplest way of obtaining a head with well defined features is to draw and cut out silhouettes of the face desired, in profile, exaggerating the projections, and then stitch the two pieces together. This gives a good nose and chin, but a seam down the middle. This may not matter for character or grotesque dolls, but for most models, this should be covered by a 'skin' of stockinet or thin cotton, which will take the shape of the profile, and can be painted with features. I used this for the *Elizabeth I* doll (see page 80) quite successfully.

THE MASK OR SOLID FACE

The most realistic results in head making are obtained when the face is cast or moulded, as nearly as possible like a human face. Most people have tried Plasticine modelling, so the principles, of kneading the block soft, shaping a rough ball, then pinching the features into place, or sticking on lumps for eyes, nose and mouth, and smoothing them into position until the join is invisible, will be familiar. A rough guide is given in

Figure 15. If you have never been initiated at school into the fascinating craft of Plasticine modelling, try it now, and you may discover a natural talent for sculpture. Apart from using your fingers, a small, not-too-sharp pointed instrument is useful for shaping the features and smoothing joins. You can buy a special tool from a craft shop, but an old steel knitting needle, or a blunted tiny screwdriver or bradawl will do just as well.

Antique dolls were made sometimes with wax faces, and it is possible to model with beeswax obtainable from candle-making shops. It should be slightly warmed, in the hands or on a radiator, shaped, and left to

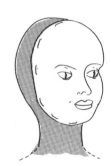

Figure 14. Face mask on cloth ball head (using Figure 3). Pierce holes near edge with sharp needle or fine drill and stitch on, or stick with glue.

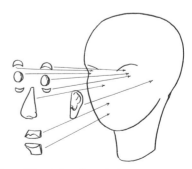

Figure 15. Moulding. Plasticine head. Attach features and smooth off edges.

set hard. It looks beautiful, but it is heavy, and can be difficult to attach to the body. But if you are really good at sculpting, you may like to try it. Either wire the head while warm, for fixing later to the trunk, or mould the whole face and head back round a core of polystyrene (Styrofoam), projecting well down into the neck, which can be stitched to the cloth, with care.

Carving faces, in balsawood, cork or fruitwood, is similarly something which may come easily to the occasional person. This is too specialised a subject for this book, but it is a talent sometimes possessed by grandfathers and little boys, so it is worth enquiring round the family for volunteers. Attach carved heads by sticking with glue.

A more usual form of solid modelled head is made of papier mâché pulp, composed of shredded paper, soaked in cellulose paste, with a plastic filler added. This is something of the consistency of porridge, and can be moulded with the fingers, or cast.

Make the pulp by boiling up, in an old saucepan, newspaper torn into tiny pieces, covered with a little water, and stirring it to a mush. The smaller the pieces, the better the finished pulp. Boil for about half an hour, and keep stirring and shredding all the time. Let it cool, and squeeze out the surplus water through a colander, and grind the whole thing up if it seems too coarse.

To make it workable add adhesive and filler. If you have made 5 oz of pulp (roughly 25 sheets of a large newspaper, shredded and boiled) add *either* $\frac{3}{4}$ oz of cellulose adhesive, or 2 oz of cold water starch paste *or* 1 oz of glue, made up to a thin jelly, and also *either* 2 oz of modelling clay *or* 1 oz of plaster and 1 oz of cellulose filler mixed. Add as little water as possible, to make a uniform mix. You can either knead the glue and fillers into the mass, or keep stirring, or, if you like to risk it, use a cake mixer at slow speed — not a blender, since the mix is not fine enough. It is a messy business to clean the mixer, but it does do the job evenly and quickly. More filler can be added, to make the mass more readily mouldable, but it will

also be more brittle when set. If you use flour paste, you will have to add a preservative.

This papier mâché pulp moulds like clay, sets overnight in a warm place, and is then very tough, and can be sandpapered to remove any roughness, painted over with a base coat of emulsion paint, then decorated with features. The head can have the body cloth stuck to it, or a wire hook can be set into the neck while wet, and the trunk wired on, for strength. The head can be modelled around a stick neck, which should be roughened first, to help adhesion.

Probably more people will feel at home with laminating a hollow mask, of the face or full head, onto a base. The first requisite is a model, either one you have made yourself by moulding Plasticine or other material, or a commercial doll's head, or a suitable face on a household ornament. Choose, or make, a face with well-defined features, for a little shape may be lost in the process of lamination. Avoid a head with moulded hair if possible. You can use the face part only, and make a head back from Plasticine.

Grease the model thoroughly, with petroleum jelly, or baby cream, or any other substance which will coat without leaving lumps, to prevent the casting from sticking to the model. If grease does not harm the model, casting will not, but, since a whole head cast needs to be cut apart with a sharp knife, you should not attempt to use a valued antique doll's head or ornament as a model, in case of scratch marks.

Stick small scraps of paper, with cellulose paste well soaked in, on the greased model (Figure 16). The paper should not be so

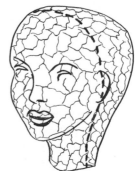

Figure 16. Lamination from head model. Use 2–3 layers of paper scraps, well overlapped. When quite dry, cut on dotted line with sharp knife. Stick paper over join, and reinforce inside and out, smoothing down outer edges carefully.

Hendrikje, Dirk and Rosa

Hans, Ladislas and Tyrolean Mädchen

Rosina, Pedro and Hattie

thick that it will not take the shape of the features, or so thin that it disintegrates. Paper tissue moulds beautifully, but, if it gets too wet, it goes soggy and slides around all over the place, sticking to the paste brush, not the model. Therefore, begin with newspaper, or the thin sort of typing paper, torn into 1 in square scraps. Smooth the pasted paper well into the feature indentations, and make two or three layers. Dry in a warm place, and, when it is quite set, ease it off the model. A face will lift away (if you have greased well) but a full head should be slit with a craft knife round the hair line and side of the neck. Fit the pieces together again and stick thin white paper over the crack.

Cover the whole head carefully with a layer of white paper, or two layers of tissue, which can be used now since it does not have to get so wet. Make sure that the new layer fits well into the feature indentations. Reinforce the inside with another layer of paper, which does not have to conform to the shape precisely. Don't make the model too wet while you are doing this. Then dry off again, and paint or decorate it with felt-tip pens. A whole head mask is then ready for use.

A face mask can be fixed to a cloth ball head, a solid pulp head, or a back-of-head cast from a separate Plasticine mould. It can be made in laminated cloth, by the same method, using thin soft muslin, or old thin sheeting. Soak a piece larger than the model in cellulose paste, and press it down firmly on a well-greased model, smoothing out all wrinkles. Stick a second pasted layer on the first, and dry off in a warm place. With care, you will be able to soak the middle of the cloth and keep the edges dry, which helps by providing an unstiffened area to stitch to the back head. This head can also be stiffened from the inside.

Lamination is easy to do, but care must be taken to mould the first layer of paper very tightly to the model's features, since each layer depends on the precision of the one below it. Fortunately, even if some definition is lost at this stage, careful painting and shadowing can give some of it back later.

Making a Plaster Mould
A more precisely moulded head can be made, with more trouble, by casting the model in plaster and making an internal mould from it. The model should be well-greased, as always, and you will need a smallish deep tray or box, 1 in bigger all round than the model.

This tray can be cardboard or thin plastic, so long as it can either be ripped off the plaster block, or bent to remove it. The thin plastic trays which supermarkets pack mushrooms and small perishables in are fine for large heads, and little sausage trays for face moulds. Freezer boxes are less flexible, so, if you use one of these, line it with paper beforehand, so that you can tip the mould out when set, and be careful the paper does not get mixed up in the plaster while you are pouring it.

Mix a little plaster of Paris — the quick-setting kind — with water, coat the bottom of the tray, and put your model in, face down. Pour plaster around it to the half-way mark, keeping it as level as possible while so doing. When it is set hard, grease or varnish the flat surface beside the model, and pour a second lot of plaster, covering the back of the head well. If your first tray is not deep enough, then turn over the model plus the half of the plaster mould, and make the second half of the mould from it in a second tray, propping it up with match-sticks, so that it doesn't sink into the wet new plaster. When the two halves are set, take them out, with the model inside, and mark or scratch a notch down two sides to show where the moulds should meet. Lift them off the model, and you now have two hollow shapes of the back and front of the head, which can be used in various ways.

Laminating or Casting from a Mould
First grease or varnish inside the hollow moulds, to prevent sticking. Then you can

laminate paste-soaked paper or cloth into the two moulds used separately, pushing the material very well down into the first layer, which is the one which will be the surface in the end, and completing the other layers, which will not show, at one go. Your pointed modelling tool will be a help in getting the first layer well into the indentations, but be careful not to gouge the plaster. If you have a good model and a neat hand, you can get really crisp faces by this method. Let the two halves dry out thoroughly, then stick them together with a band of paper or cloth.

Alternatively, make a solid or semi-solid head of papier mâché pulp, pressing it down very firmly into the face mould. A solid head is made by filling two half moulds completely, and sticking the halves together when dry. A less heavy one can be made by leaving a hollow depression in each side. In both cases insert a piece of wire in each side while the work is wet, or insert a loop later. The surface of the papier mâché can be improved by coating with a thin paste of the filler.

There are a number of proprietary compounds sold for modelling, which are claimed to mould like Plasticine, yet set 'in a few hours' like plaster. Obviously, this would be ideal for making heads, but those which I have so far tried don't mould very well, crumble apart, and take a week to set. I mention them because there is no good scientific reason why an efficient compound should not appear on the market any day. If anyone has found such a thing, I would be pleased to hear of it. If such a material does arrive, remember to set a wire loop in the neck during modelling, for attaching the head to the trunk later.

The two moulds can be clamped together, or tied with string, and used for poured casting. If the moulds are coated with silicone release agent, then plaster can be poured into the plaster mould, through the neck hole, remembering to insert a wire for attaching the head to the body. If the plaster is agitated a little during the pouring to remove bubbles, it will take shape beautifully, and set to a fine ceramic appearance. The plaster head can be painted and varnished and looks splendid — but it *weighs* very heavy, and is difficult to support, even with wires. It is also brittle, and small projections, like noses, tend to snap off when it is handled.

Remeltable rubber, sold in craft shops, makes a lovely head, with good features, and a pleasantly surfaced skin. However, for reasons best known to themselves, the manufacturers add heavy pigments, red and yellow ochre. I have yet to find a paint which will coat these colours without crazing, due to the flexibility of the moulds. But if you can think of a use for a model with an ochre skin, this is for you.

Epoxy resin can also be used for moulded heads. A clear resin is sold in craft shops "for casting" and is intended for embedding ornaments in transparent film. Avoid this, since it is expensive, and takes a week to set. Use instead the opaque kind sold, more cheaply, for repairing cars and boats, as fibre glass resin. It comes in two containers, a base and a hardener, and once A is mixed with B, it starts to set rock hard, so do not make up more than you can use in half an hour. Mix cold, pour the goo in through the neck of the mould — then insert a wire for attaching it — and leave to set for a few hours, to make sure the middle of the cast is hard.

This material, though mixed cold, is inflammable, so don't smoke while using it. Also it has a disgusting sickly smell (to me, at least), so it is best to work outside, or with an open window. When set, however, the resin cast does not smell at all. If any resin spills, mop it up right away, since it bonds hard to a number of surfaces. Work over newspaper, and use a discardable paper cup and ice lolly stick for mixing.

The surface of the cast may be a bit grainy, but it can be sandpapered to a fine finish, as on cars. It can be painted with cellulose paint, used for children's toy models and some cars, or acrylic paint, from craft shops.

FACES

Faces can be embroidered or appliquéd on cloth heads, and drawn in felt-tip pen or painted on almost all surfaces of heads used. Unless you are an artistic genius with a talent for miniature work, keep the features simple, suggesting rather than blocking in the details. Try out shapes and colours on paper and cloth first. When you are satisfied with the effect, transfer to the face. Work in a good light, and ignore the doorbell and 'phone. A tiny mistake can be removed with the appropriate paint solvent on a tiny tissue, but unless you have the touch of an angel, think twice, since a slip can spread a sludge of messy paint over perfectly good painting. If the error is a tiny blob, will it really show? If it will, how about turning it into a black beauty spot? If there is a thin smear, let it dry, and paint over in base colour.

Aim for simplicity, as cartoonists do in getting their effects. Unless you are making a deliberate grotesque, like a witch or devil, play down the expression. A faint smile is easier to live with for long than a mad grin, and the costumes will add a great deal of personality to the wearer. If a face lacks something, you can always add later. If it has too much, there is little to be done about it.

Whenever possible, have the main skin areas tinted before the doll is made up. Large tracts of paint tend to crack, and it is hard to get the subtle skin shades by surface tinting anyway. Dye the cloth for several dolls at once, in the piece, using bought dyes, or, since these are often out of stock when you want them, experiment with household materials. Cold tea, tinted to a pinker shade with cochineal or raspberry juice, can produce an acceptable Anglo-Saxon skin. The shade can be deepened by the number of times the cloth is steeped in the dye vat. Onion skin produces the yellowish tinge used, not for Chinese and Japanese, who can be whiter than 'white' people, but for Eskimos, and, in combination with tea, Indo-Chinese, Malays, etc.

'Black' skin is usually some shade of brown, for actual black dye tends to be too dull to show the right sheen on even the darkest face. For special effects, a fine black skin with life and gloss to it can be made of nylon velvet, drawn over a profile head, or cut as a *Rag Rosy* head. The lips and bright teeth have to be painted on, also the eyes.

Society ladies in the seventeenth and eighteenth centuries made up their faces with a white, arsenic-based powder, so make their skins very pale indeed, with staring patches of red rouge on their cheeks. The male courtiers were just as made up, so use this white and rouge combination for them also, if you are prepared to explain to the curious. As mentioned earlier, many of the ladies' costumes were very off the shoulder. So, to avoid showing seams in the dolls, you should cut a second skin in satin, from a hollow circle or oval of cloth, and appliqué it over the shoulders. The join at the neck can be hidden by a neckband or necklace. There may be enough give in the cloth to fit around the shoulders in one piece, or any adjustment can be made at the back. Kid can also be used for this purpose, and even eased out to make noses, etc., with a little judicious damping and pressing over a finger or mould. Chamois softens when wet, and can be moulded. Don't forget that, where arms and legs show, they need to be tinted as well, if your doll hasn't an all-over 'skin' colour.

I have not tried to dictate styles of facial features, because this is something which every one works out for himself, and no two people seem to use the same techniques, or achieve the same results. This is the essence of making individual dolls, not factory facsimiles. A little practice first, on paper, will show you what you are capable of, and what to avoid. The cardinal rule is: Keep it Simple — and go ahead.

HAIR

Doll's hair can be made from more or less anything which can be arranged in strands or curls — embroidery silk or cotton, wool, fur, fur fabric, string, plumber's hemp, leather strips, horsehair stuffing, sheep wool, unravelled sweaters — and, best of all, theatrical crêpe hair. There is also doll's hair, as sold in craft shops, which is crêpe hair at twice the price. The only thing which won't work at all well is human hair (except the very frizzy sort). Most human hair slides about, won't stick, won't style, won't curl, and somehow doesn't look very realistic. Choose your kind of hair according to the type of doll. Grotesque dolls look fine with 'fun' hair, but not society ladies.

The hair can be applied by sewing, sticking, or as a wig. Cloth headed dolls can have their hair stitched to them directly, using embroidery silk or cotton, for fine work, and wool or, with care, teased-out string, for coarse work. Embroidery thread looks best for styles with smooth flat hair, close to the head or tightly plaited. The basic method for stitched hair is to work in two main lines — across the crown, and on top of the head with a parting. Figures 17 a and b show the layout for straight hair, unstyled, with the direction of the stitches. The hair can be short or long, by changing the length of the loops, and kept level by working the loops round a card or stick, fixed at the desired length. Cut the ends of the loops when the hair is all on, and tie back the sides.

If the hair is to be short and tidy, this layout is less suitable, since the ends will not hang neatly. Therefore, draw an outline of the required hairline, in light pencil, $\frac{1}{8}$ in inside its limit, and work the thread in and out just covering the line. Figures 18 a and b show the lay of the threads, with no thread wasted by running under the cloth. A certain number of stitches are necessary to cover the hairline over the ears. A side parting is similarly done, but extra stitches are then necessary at one side and the front of the hairline (Figures 18 c and d).

Plaits are done with the same top layout as for loose hair, but, since there is an additional back parting revealed by the style, this is stitched like the top, with a small filling in of hair across the back crown line (Figures 19 a

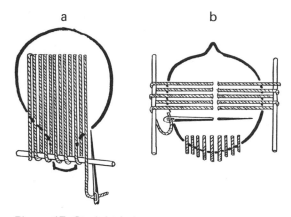

a   b

Figure 17. Straight hair.
(a) Back view. (b) Top of head, with centre parting. Hold rod firmly at the desired length, and wind each strand round with even tension. Remove rod and cut loops when enough hair is attached.

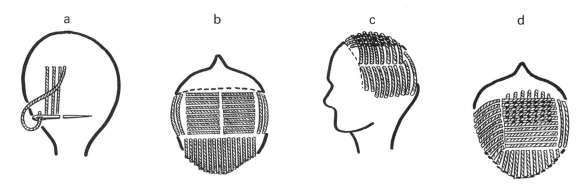

a   b   c   d

Figure 18. Short cropped hair.
(a) Back view. (b) Top of head. Centre parting with side hair. Draw in dotted hairline, and work just over this. (c) Side parting. Add short lengths to fill in top hair line and (d) the other side.

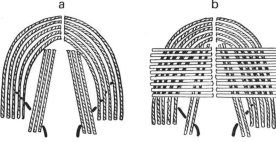

a b

Figure 19. Plaits.
*Wind ends round slanted rod to keep lengths
even and cut loops. Comb back into two halves,
on either side of central parting. Divide each
into three sections and plait. Secure with rubber
band and wool ribbon.*

and b). A few stitches above the ears are also
required.

Small, tight, sausage curls can be made
by placing a thin rod (a knitting needle, say)
against the head, and stitching round it and
through a small portion of the cloth (Figure
20). Remove the rod when five or six turns
are complete, and make a securing stitch.
Thick rods give fatter, loose curls. A more
solid curl can be made over a pad of cotton
wool, left in place.

Figure 20. Curls.
*Stitch separately at ends of fixed hair (as Figure
18) or while laying on hair, taking a short stitch
into the head fabric. Curls to be fixed to a solid
head should be made as in Figure 24.*

Crêpe hair, or other non-thread materials,
can be applied in the same way to a cloth
head, stitching it on across the back crown,
then in a flat hank on top of the head. The
stitching line forms the parting (Figure 21).

Figure 21. Attaching crêpe
hair.
*Stitch firmly to head or wig
base with line of back-stitch
in matching cotton. Steam
crêpe hair to straighten
section of hank. Baste
invisibly at sides and back of
head.*

This is the best way to fix string, hemp or
unravelled wool.

A short hairstyle can in some cases be
made from fur or fur fabric, shaped in a cap
to the head. The dimensions will vary according to the head of the model, but normally,
you will need two pieces, one for the back
crown, either round or oval in shape, and
one strip to fit the top and sides (Figure 22).
Cut the fur or fabric by pushing thin, sharp
scissors through the back, and cutting carefully to avoid squashing the pile, and oversew
the skins, or make the smallest seam in the
fabric, taking care not to tangle the pile in
the stitching. Sew or stick the cap of fur to
the head, and brush the pile forward over the
hairline.

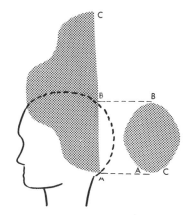

Figure 22. Fur cap.
*Adapt dimensions to fit head used exactly.
Stitch on wrong side, stick cap to head, and
brush edges of fur forward to conceal join.*

In some cases, the hat or headdress will
cover all the hair, or nearly all. If so, the
head could be merely painted with hair, and
tiny strands or ringlets attached to the hairline, or to the actual headdress.

Solid heads can have crêpe hair directly
stuck onto them, but care must be taken to
conceal the glue lines. The row across the
back crown is done normally, since the
front hair conceals the glue, but the hair at the
top must be glued in the reverse direction. For
a drawn back style, glue the hair $\frac{1}{2}$ in inside
the natural hairline, so that it hangs down
over the face, then turn it back in a loose wave

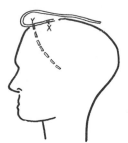

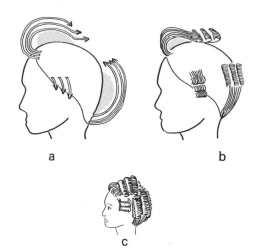

Figure 23. Reverse hair. Attach firmly inside hairline at (x) by stitching or glue. Tack down lightly on hairline (y) and fold back in gentle curve over top of head.

a

b

c

Figure 25. Pompadour wig.
The style is best made on a muslin cap base, using white crêpe hair or embroidery silk. (a) Attach top and back hair in reverse direction, turning back over cotton-wool pads. (b) Attach curls and ringlets where shown. (c) Finished wig.

(Figure 23). For a parted style, glue it ½ in from the parting lines, pointing the 'wrong' way, and bend back at the parting line — or lay a flat hank of hair across the top of the head, and stick the underside of it only. This method is used on some cheap commercial dolls, but is not very satisfactory, since bits of hair tend to escape, or blobs of glue show through.

It is better to make a wig cap, on the same lines as the fur cap (Figure 22), and stitch the hair to it. Use a base of tinted cloth, or muslin, either pale gold or brown. Stitch a line of hair across the back crown, and, for a drawn back style, another reversed inside the front hairline, turning the hank back in a soft wave (as Figure 23). This will be quite securely fixed, and can be invisibly basted to make several styles. Elaborate variations can be made by altering the placing of the hanks of hair, and curls can be formed, with the ends of the hanks, using a rod, as above. Hanging ringlets can be attached to the cap wig, if the hair is curled round a rod, on a base of tissue paper, which is then torn away, leaving a line of stitching, which can be secured to the main wig (Figure 24). A complicated Pompadour wig, with padding to give height, is shown in Figure 25 a and b.

Bald heads can be made on a cap of pink satin or tinted cloth, with the hair thinly stitched, in reverse direction, around the receding hairline, and turned to cover it, then lightly stitched into place. If you are making a partly receding style, like that of *Prince Albert* (see page 95), follow the layout in Figure 26.

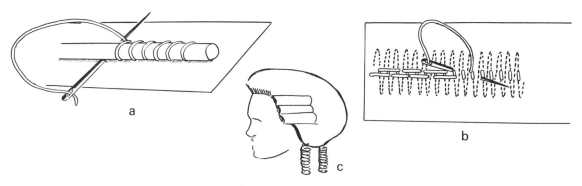

a

b

c

Figure 24. Ringlets.
(a) Place rod on piece of tissue and stitch through a section of paper each time. (b) Turn over and baste down ringlet with two lines of stitches, through hair and paper. (c) Tear off surplus paper and attach to main wig. Crêpe hair can be rolled into cylinders and secured from the back in the same way.

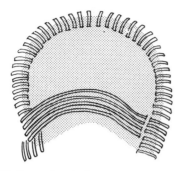

Figure 26. Receding hair.
Work on skin-coloured cap, stitching neatly from curved hairline round crown, or used reversed crêpe hair. Cover join of cap and forehead with draped strands of hair or lines of wrinkles.

In most cases, the finished wig can be sewn or stuck into place, keeping glue well away from the hairline. A bald wig, for an old man, can have a shaded line of 'wrinkles' to cover the join, but, in the case of a younger man, like *Albert*, the face skin should be continued up over the natural hairline in front, and the wig cap made to start behind it. The join will then be covered by the top-knot of hair.

CHAPTER 4

Materials and Accessories

Everything used in dressing your doll has to be scaled down in size, to give the right effect. If patterned fabric is needed, then the repeated design must be on a small scale, unless a vulgar or deliberately dramatic effect is wanted. The tiny floral or spotted patterns used for traditional baby dresses may look dull on the infant, but they are perfect for a doll. Just occasionally, a really large motif on a plain ground will make a grand effect if it happens to be the right size for a whole section of a garment. Textured materials often look very impressive in small pieces. Assess the effect by folding part of the fabric up to the right size for a dress etc, and holding it against the doll figure, or anything the same size.

MATERIALS AND HEMS

The thickness of the material is important, for all fabrics appear to be relatively bulkier, in contrast with the doll figure, than on a person. Even though the waist is cut narrow, to allow for the thickness of the clothing, any attempt to use the authentic kind of material would produce a walking barrel, rather than a doll. Our ancestors dressed in thick wool, coarse linen and heavy velvet to keep out wind and weather. These should be simulated in thinner fabrics which give the same effect on a small scale. For rough wool, for cloaks and breeches, it is best to substitute felt or a wool and cotton mixture, not thin wool, which does not hang stiffly enough, and tends to fray. Fine wool, for dresses, is replaced by thick cotton or rayon, and plush or thick velvet by thin nylon velvet.

Very thin fabrics do pose a problem, though. On a society lady, a transparent, gauzy scarf or fichu would show tantalising glimpses of dainty shoulders and bosom. On a doll, unless draped carefully, they may show lumpy side seams. Therefore, either use thin, but opaque, cloth, or cover the upper body of the doll with a cast or carefully cut and stitched appliquéd shoulder and bosom in fine cloth, satin or kid, or a stretchy material, so that the joins do not show.

One big difficulty is finishing the edges of the garments, since hems which are small by normal standards look like thick lumps on dolls. Non-fraying materials, like felt, leather and plastic, can be used un-hemmed for some purposes, and the kind of loosely woven material which unravels so badly that it needs a broad hem to control it should be avoided. Close-woven materials can often be held in place with tiny stitches which scarcely show on the right side. Where they do go through, it may be possible to cover them with minute embroidery, or trimming. Machine stitched hems look quite wrong, and should only be used where they are to be covered by braid or embroidered edging. Fortunately, the clothes do not come under the constant strain of dressing and undressing, so quite light hems may be enough to hold them. Where there are several layers of clothes coinciding at a point, such as the waist, it may be possible to stagger the joins, or to baste the under-layers flat to the upper layer, which is then hemmed over them, to avoid the bulk of several hems in one place. For narrow bands or inserts of material, you may find a ribbon of the right colour, to avoid two closely occurring hems.

Use of Bits and Pieces

One of the great virtues of doll making is that it is a miniature craft, and so can make use of little bits and pieces which would otherwise be wasted. Small pieces of material left over from other sewing will make a whole dress for a doll. Outgrown baby clothes, with their small-scale patterns, and old evening dresses which unaccountably have ceased to meet round their owner can clothe several dolls, and have happy memories built in to them as well. Even household calamities can be put to use. The one glove remaining of a pair will make shoes, hats, and, if pale coloured, skin for off-the-shoulder beauties. Odd socks and laddered tights make hose, and old sweaters can be cut up for stuffing, or unravelled to make hair.

Old sheeting is a commodity most families have in quantity, and this is very useful. The strongest parts can be dyed and used for bodies, and the thin bits for laminated masks, since they will absorb the paste well, and shape easily. Most dolls need layers of white undergarments too.

The secret of being a really well equipped doll maker is hoarding. Keep a box, or several boxes, and stow away everything which might be useful. Rough sort them into types of cloth, braids, and trimmings, then you will be able to track them down when you need them. Scraps of ribbon, lace, braid, upholstery trimmings, wool, embroidered motifs, small buttons, beads, brooches and loose stones from them, sequins and buckles — all will be useful, sorted into packets for tidiness.

Do not forget the metal foil and shiny wrappings from chocolates and Christmas goodies. The tiny tassels and ornaments from fancy packs are ideal for dolls. Bottle corks, and interesting shaped plastic bottles, cardboard, small scraps of wire, parcel string, mostly come free, or as incidentals to something else. Don't save aerosol cans, which could explode, or tins which will corrode, but almost anything else is potential raw material. In the country, feathers from your friendly neighbourhood chicken or ducks, sheep wool, horse hair and garden twigs can be there for the collecting. Walnut shells for funny faces, oak galls for tiny dolls' heads, long straw for plaiting — anything could be useful. Never throw anything away without thinking, and you will not be faced with buying a yard of ribbon when you need four inches.

You may end up with the most cluttered house in the street, but your dustbin will be the tidiest in town. Anyway, governments are spending millions studying the recycling of packaging material, which you have, after a fashion, achieved by your own efforts!

What You Need to Buy

In spite of saving everything available, you will need to buy, at some time, sewing cottons in all colours; embroidery silk or cotton as needed; crêpe hair from theatrical or novelty suppliers; thin felt in various colours (art shops and fabric stores); thin wire for body frameworks (gardening shops); Plasticine, felt-tip pens and paints (art shops, department stores); cellulose paste and glue, plaster of Paris (household stores); kapok or cotton wool (drugstores, furniture shops, chemists) ; and dowelling for stiffening necks (timber merchants/hardware stores). If you run out of white lace recovered from underwear, buy it in rolls from wholesale suppliers, and use upholstery braid, sold for fixing chairs and cushions, rather than the dress quality of gold braid, which costs the earth. You will need a good pair of sharp scissors, with an extra pair of tiny ones, for snipping around the fiddly bits of the work. A spike-pointed needle for sewing leather, and a thin sharp needle for fine cloth will also be useful.

In the specifications for some of the historical dolls, I have been lavish in my use of 'jewels'. These can be little stones prised off old brooches, or beads from an old necklace. The tiny seed pearls (fake) which don't look much on a person, are fabulous on a doll. If you need more than you have around, then buy a cheap bit of costume jewellery from a street market, or invest in a few dozen glass sparklers, which can be bought very cheaply from wholesale jewellers, who supply the factories which make cheap costume jewellery. The small cost is more than offset by the splendid effect of the 'rubies', 'emeralds' and 'diamonds' on the doll.

CHAPTER 5

Which Fabrics and Stitches?

In the following pages, there are patterns and descriptions for dressing both national and historical dolls. I have assumed that at least some of the readers of this book will be first-time doll makers, with not much experience of sewing, but if you happen to be a mother who has made every stitch of clothing for fourteen children I hope that you will forgive me. Some terms I use repeatedly, and I have explained them here, rather than go into details each time they arise. I shall give suggestions for fabrics and colours to be used, so that you can vary them according to what you have available, keeping to the general description of dark or light, bright or pastel, silky or matt.

FABRICS

Sateen always means a cotton cloth woven with a shiny finish, resembling satin. *Cotton* even thin cotton, is always opaque, whereas *muslin* is a thin, soft, semi-transparent cloth.

Figured muslin is semi-transparent, but stiff, with a woven or embroidered pattern, usually vaguely floral, in thin lines on it. *Organdie* is sheer, stiff fabric, usually plain, but sometimes patterned like figured muslin. *Paper nylon* is very similar, a stiff, matt nylon.

Stockinet is slightly elastic, with a flat woven surface on one side, not the loose ribbed knit used for cleaning cloths. *Felt* is always thin, never slipper grade.

STITCHES USED IN THIS BOOK
Joining stitches
a. *Basting* or *Tacking:* Even-running stitches

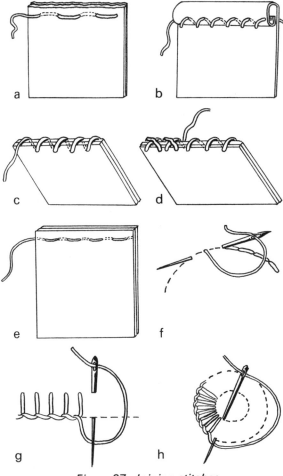

Figure 27. Joining stitches.

to join loosely edges not under strain, or due to be finished with braid or embroidery.

b. *Hemming:* For firm edging. Turn under minimum amount, on the wrong side, and conceal hems by taking tiniest possible stitch through to right side.

c. *Oversewing:* Small, firm, diagonal stitches, for joining felt, fur, etc. Can be worked on right or wrong side.

d. *Double Oversew* or *Cross-stitch:* Second line of stitches as (c) above, back across first row. Used where felt is to be turned inside out after joining. Worked loosely, gives a flat edge.

e. *Stab Stitch:* To join felt or leather edge that is intended to remain parallel. Same action as basting, but smaller stitches, made singly, not in runs.

f. *Backstitch:* Each stitch covers half the length of former stitch. Makes a straight firm line, continuous back and front.

g. *Blanket Stitch:* Binds two fraying edges, where hem would be too bulky. Baste or backstitch first, on wrong side of work.

h. *Buttonhole-stitch:* Same action, but worked much closer together in straight line for firm edge, in oval or circle for simulated buttonhole or button.

Decorative stitches

i. *Stem Stitch:* Worked as backstitch, over two spaces at a time, but overlapped slightly, giving a jagged line.

j. *Cross-stitch:* Either as in (d) above, or worked individually. Start at top left, cross to bottom right, take thread under and back to bottom left, cross over to top right. Then take thread underneath to bottom left of next stitch, up to top right, under and back to top left, cross over to bottom left, and so on, alternately.

k. *Herring-bone:* On the same principle as cross-stitch, but the top of each stitch crosses the one before. Can be worked closely for mass effect.

l. *Chain-stitch:* Worked in loops along a notional centre line. Make stitch through back of work, twist thread around the needle

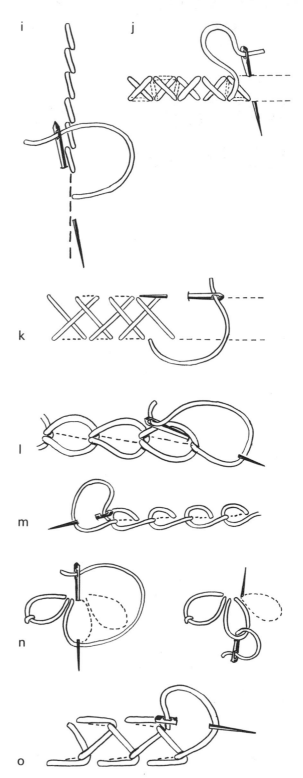

Figure 28. Simple decorative stitches.

36

point, and pull through, not too tightly.
Insert needle in loop, adjacent to previous
exit hole; take the same length of stitch, and
twist thread around point again from same
direction each time.

m. *Open Chain:* The same principle as chain-
stitch, but the needle is inserted, not inside
the first loop, but halfway along the second
one, for subsequent stitches. Useful narrow
edging stitch.

n. *Lazy Daisy:* Each chain loop is held down
by a tiny retaining bar stitch. Worked in
circles to make stylised daisy flower.

o. *Feather stitch:* Work between two notional parallel lines. Bring needle out on
bottom line. Insert on top line, directly above
first exit hole, leaving thread loose, bring
point of needle out a short distance ahead.
Loop thread under needle before drawing
through. Reinsert point in bottom line,
directly below previous exit hole, keeping
thread loose ; come out a short distance ahead
and continue as above. Keep stitch length
even and make alternate loops at top and
bottom line.

p. *Zigzag:* This is a splayed out chain stitch,
worked in rows or groups. Start at left of
work, and insert the needle point about
$\frac{1}{4}$ in away along same line, bringing the
point out halfway between these positions,
in upper line, and looping the thread around
before pulling through. Anchor stitch with a
tiny retaining bar, bringing thread out just
next to bottom right of a completed stitch,
to start the next stitch, in line with the first.

q. *Lozenge:* A second row of zigzags,
inverted, under the first row, makes lozenges.

r. *Honeycomb:* A third row, or more, of
zigzags, in staggered lines after the first pair.

s. *Fir-tree:* An ascending ladder of zigzags,
in diminishing sizes, with a longer retaining
bar to form the trunk, and cross-stitches to
finish top and base.

t. *Long-short stitch:* Simple straight stitches,
arranged in circular patterns, make a stylised
flower of the chrysanthemum type.

u. and v. *Satin-stitch:* A flower or leaf, outlined in basting stitches, stitched with closely
packed straight stitches, all in one direction

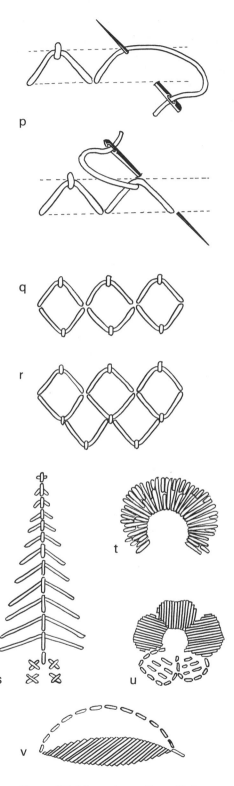

Figure 29. More decorative stitches.

37

for one part of the design. It can be given plumpness by padding with small running stitches underneath, in opposite direction. Used for roses, and glossy petalled flowers.

w. to y. *Beaufort stitch:* To decorate Tudor garments of *Henry VIII*. (w) Make line of zigzag stitches, held down by tiny chain-stitch loops instead of plain bar. Repeat with inverted line to form lozenge. (x) Cross lozenges with widely spaced row of herring-bone, in second colour, with terminal holes well outside the line of the retaining loops. All crossing threads should be run under the lozenges. (y) Make a second row of herring-bone stitches, terminals level with retaining loops, woven in and out of existing stitches, over lozenge bars and under previous herring-bone bars.

The finished stitch is contained mostly within the strips of velvet forming the doublet, with the projecting section of the first herring-bone forming half of the lozenge shape connecting one strip with another (see figure 103).

PATTERNS

The patterns given on the following pages are full size, unless indicated. Minor variations in length, etc. are described in the text, and slight alterations to a basic pattern are shown in diagram form, to be drawn out in the full size. Measurements are all in inches. In some cases, instructions are given to alter the basic size of the doll body. This, or

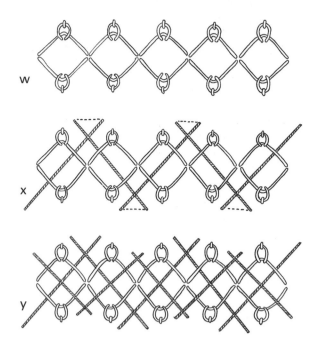

Figure 30. Beaufort stitch.

individual differences in the amount of stuffing used, may make a slight adjustment necessary in the clothes pattern size, which is for an average doll.

Read all the instructions for the doll you wish to make before you start, then cut out the patterns to be used in card or stiff paper. Label them on the back with the name of the doll and the pattern piece, and transfer all cutting notes and marks written on the original to the copy. They can be kept in sets in an old envelope, for future use.

CHAPTER 6

Dressing your First Doll

If you are making and dressing a doll for the first time, then you will probably find it easiest to start with a *Rag Rosy*. Full instructions for making her up are given in Chapter Two. If you prefer to make the flat-faced version, *Fanny*, the same considerations apply. The stitching together of the all-in-one head and body is quick and easy, so that you will not be long delayed in getting started with the actual dressing. *Fanny* is the simplest of all, because there are no head darts, but putting her hair on is a little more awkward than for *Rosy*, though, because her finished head is flat, not ball shaped.

PEASANT COSTUMES

The simplest doll's costume to make, which can be finished in an afternoon, is a *Peasant Girl*. If you look at pictures of costumes from Europe alone, you will see a bewildering variety of colours, trimmings, embroideries and styles, but the basic ideas behind almost all the women's costumes are the same. The ordinary folk, not the fashionable rich, or the ragged poor, wore clothes which were warm, easy to work in, and didn't show the dirt too much, because washing thick clothing and drying it wasn't easy for most of the year. Most of the clothes were quite attractive too, and the Sunday trimmings added to them were very attractive.

The basic garment was a big loose skirt, worn over one, two, or, in the colder countries, up to seven petticoats. The upper body was covered with a chemise, or loose blouse of thin material, and with a bodice in thicker cloth, sometimes attached to the skirt, but usually separate. Only the chemise, and the under-petticoat were washed often, and the skirt was kept reasonably clean by an apron over it.

As well as these basic clothes, there were shoulder scarves or shawls to keep off the chill air of evening, and sleeved jackets or capes to ward off winter cold. On the feet, at any rate in the cooler countries, were worn slippers for indoor use, and buckled shoes or boots for walking to church on Sunday. Wooden clogs were worn by farm girls who had to wade through the yard, and by most people in marshy Holland. Socks and stockings were coarse wool, woven or knitted, often at home.

Most of the other things worn were trimmings, not essential parts of the costume. An exception was the head covering, which did keep off the sun or wind, but was mostly worn for reasons of modesty, and to show which girls were married and which were single. Young girls wore little caps of lace or muslin, until they married, after which it was proper to cover most of their hair, and some of their face, from all men except their husbands. The caps were different from place to place, and often very elaborate, especially for Sunday.

In the long winter evenings, the women passed the time by decorating their clothes, with embroidery, or ribbon braiding, and made little frilly nonsenses, like muslin aprons, to replace, or go over the work-a-day one. These varied from place to place, and make the costumes look very different, on top, but the general shape is the same, underneath.

Rosa (Plate 1)

Our peasant girl, *Rosa*, comes from 'Mittel Europa,' has blonde plaits, a lace cap, a chemise, a warm bodice, one petticoat, a coloured skirt, two aprons, white stockings, black shoes — and pantaloons, though they were not worn, for warmth or modesty, until the nineteenth century, even by rich ladies. *Rosa* will wear them, partly because they look pretty, and partly because, if she doesn't, someone will surely think you just haven't bothered with the underwear.

To make her you will need:

  One *Rag Rosy* (or *Flat Fanny*) made up as in Chapter Two
  White cotton for pants, petticoat, chemise and one apron
  Black felt for bodice and shoes
  Black sateen for the other apron (small scrap)
  Coloured cotton for skirt
  Child's white rayon sock top, for stockings
  Lace trimming, ribbon
  Embroidery thread — red for chemise, black for bodice lacing, and gold for hair.

Cut the stocking pattern, (Figure 31) twice, from an old sock top. Stitch back and bottom seam, turn inside out, and pull over doll's foot. They will come half-way up the thigh, and can be basted into place. Cut the pantaloon pattern, twice, from white cotton (Figure 32). Make a tiny hem at top and bottom of both pieces, then, folding each section in half, lengthways, stitch the leg seams on the wrong side. Place the two legs together, and join the whole back seam on the wrong side, and the front seam from A–B. Turn the garment to the right side, and trim the bottoms of the legs with narrow white lace, gathered slightly to make a frill. Dress the doll in the pantaloons, and stitch the

Note
All basic patterns are used for several characters. They are designed for averagely stuffed Rag Rosy dolls. Loose-woven material or tighter stuffing may affect doll size. When used for wired dolls (Charles and Charlotte) add $\frac{1}{2}$ in in length and adjust width if necessary.

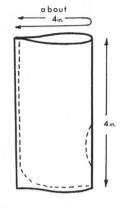

Figure 31. Stocking (basic). Cut in flexible stockinet, unless directed, and adjust to size of doll.

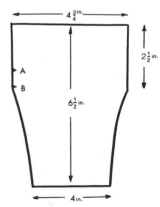

Figure 32. Pantaloons (basic). Adjust width and length according to instructions in text.

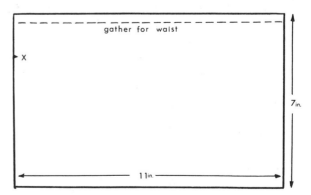

Figure 33. Petticoat (basic). Adjust according to text.

rest of the front seam, overlapping the fronts and turning in the raw edge. The front should be flat, and the rear of the garment slightly full. Take two tiny tucks in the back waistline to fit it, leaving loose pleats below. This gives a kind of bustle effect.

Cut the petticoat in white cotton, to the dimensions in Figure 33, and hem the raw edges, with the least turnover possible. Join side seam to X, turn the garment, and gather the waistline to fit the doll. Put the petticoat on, and stitch the rest of the side seam together.

Cut the chemise in the same white cotton, or a finer, thin muslin, from the patterns in Figure 34 a–c. Hem the lower edge as narrowly as possible, then turn in a hem round the neckline almost $\frac{1}{4}$ in deep when finished. Stitch side and shoulder seams of the chemise, leaving the back open for the moment. Stitch the side seam of the sleeves and gather the top to fit the armhole. With right sides together, stitch the sleeves into the armholes. Hem the bottom of the sleeve with a $\frac{1}{4}$ in hem. Now gather the neck of the chemise, from the back of the shoulder across the front to the back of the other shoulder, leaving the back of the neck smooth. The gathering stitch should run just below the line of the hem. Also gather the sleeve at the wrist, next to the hemline. Try the chemise on the doll, and adjust the gathers if necessary. When the neck fits neatly, embroider around it, and the wrist, on top of the line of gathers. Any edging stitch will do, from two rows of chain stitch upwards. I prefer herringbone or feather-stitch, both of which look folksy and are quick to do. They are included in the list of stitches given in Chapter Five. Use a bright colour, like red, blue or green, toning it with the skirt material you are using.

According to the thickness of the chemise material, it may be necessary to gather a very short length of the centre front hem at the bottom, to keep it tidy, but thinner material will fold naturally under the bodice when made. Put the finished garment on the doll from the front, overlap the back sections,

and oversew neatly into place. Finish the line of embroidery across the back neck.

The skirt is made in the same way as the petticoat, from the same pattern, cut $\frac{1}{2}$ in larger all round. Any firm piece of cotton material will do, in a plain or textured fabric, and in a bright colour to complement the black and white of the rest of the outfit. When you gather the waistline, ease most of the fullness to the back and hips, and the whole skirt will bell out behind in a saucy way.

The bodice is cut from black felt, which is flexible enough to hug the figure, and will not ravel on the edges (which cuts out the need for more tiny hems). Cut the back in one piece and the front in two (Figures 35 a and b). Stitch the side seams and one shoulder seam. Because the bodice fits more tightly than the chemise, it is difficult to slip it on over both arms when made up, and the felt is liable to tear if strained. Put it on from one side, and then stitch up the second shoulder neatly. The bodice should fit closely at the back, and the two edges should come within $\frac{1}{2}$ in of meeting at the front. Stitch the two fronts together loosely, using thick black embroidery silk, or thin black cord, criss-crossed from side to side, as in Figure 36, and tied in a small bow at the end. Narrow black ribbon might be used instead.

Rosa's under apron is an oblong of black sateen, 4 in × 2 in, tiny-hemmed all round the raw edges, and basted at the top to a 10 in length of ribbon. Trim the bottom of the apron with three lines of coloured embroidery, two thin ones sandwiching one thick, or a coloured strip of ribbon, flanked by thin embroidery (Figure 37).

Her upper apron is sheer frivolity, made of a scrap of muslin, 2 in × 1 in, edged with a white lace frill, gathered at the waist on to a narrow white ribbon. Her cap is made of a 2 in diameter circle of white cotton (cut by rounding off a 2 in square) joined to a $8\frac{1}{4}$ in × $1\frac{1}{2}$ in strip and edged with lace (Figure 38) closely gathered to make a frill. Make tiny hems at the back, and the bottom of the strip.

Rosa's face is painted or drawn in felt pen, as a naïve young girl, with a 'butter-

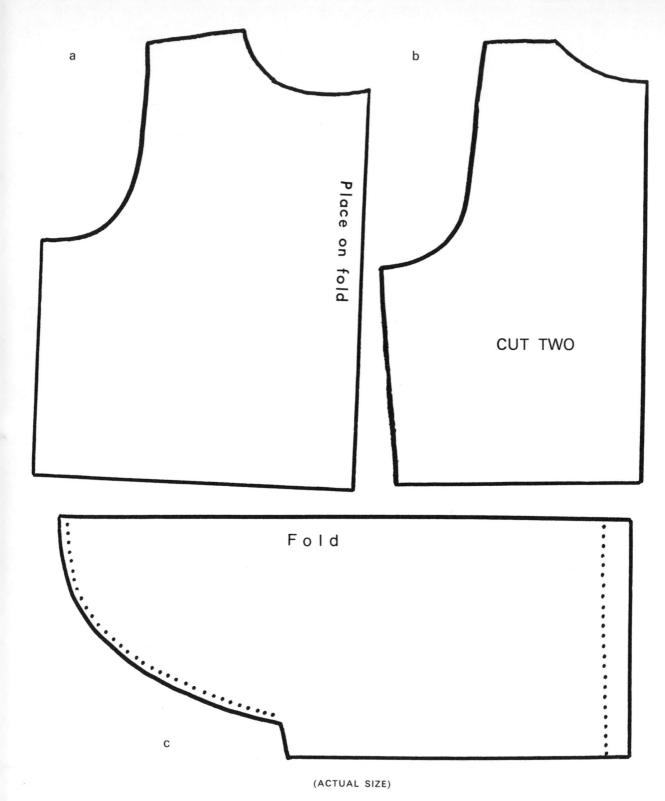

Place on fold

CUT TWO

Fold

(ACTUAL SIZE)

Figure 34. Chemise (basic).
(a) front (b) back (c) sleeve. Adjust according to text.

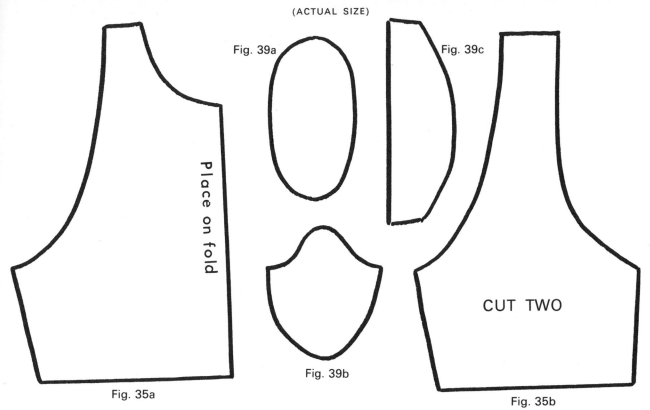

Fig. 39a

Fig. 39c

Place on fold

CUT TWO

Fig. 35a

Fig. 39b

Fig. 35b

Figure 35. Bodice (basic).
(a) Back (b) Front. Sized for felt. Add turnings for cloth.

Figure 36. Cross lacing.
Eyelet holes may be made with eyelet pliers, or simulated with a circle of button-hole stitch.

Figure 37. Apron embroidery.

$8\frac{1}{4}$ in.

$1\frac{1}{2}$ in.

2 in.

Figure 38. Bonnet (basic).
Adjust size for dolls with moulded heads.

Figure 39. Shoes (basic).
Cut in felt, oversew edges or right side. Join (a) sole to (b) toe, stiffen with card insole, and pad with stuffing. Stitch on back of heel piece (c), fit to leg, and baste sides and front of instep, stuffing any gaps.

wouldn't-melt-in-her-mouth' look. Her hair can be made from crêpe hair or embroidery silk, and set in two plaits, according to the directions in Chapter Three. Make the hair waist-length, plait it to hang behind her, and tie it with a ribbon or coloured wool bow.

Make the shoes (Figures 39 a to c) in black felt. Oversew the toe to the sole, with seams on the outside. Stiffen with card, and stuff the toe hard with kapok, or shaped cork or wood. Fit the heel piece round the ankle, and attach the sole, adding stuffing if necessary, to make the whole foot firm.

Peasant Variations
The methods of construction given for *Rosa* are basic ones and even the patterns can be used over and over again, with minor

43

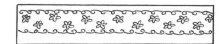

variations, mostly in the trimmings, to produce what look like different dolls. Here are a few of them.

Tyrolean Mädchen (Plate 2)

Make the pantaloons and petticoat, as before, and add a second white muslin petticoat (paper nylon is a reasonable substitute), edged with lace, or cut with pinking shears and left unhemmed. Cut the chemise with sleeves shortened to elbow length, and trim them with lace instead of embroidering. Embroider the neck as before, in blue or gold. Make the skirt in a light apple green, and the bodice in a patterned fabric, preferably blue with a white small floral pattern, or white dots. Other colours which would suit are yellow or pink grounds with white flowers or dots — the idea being to produce a light, early-summer effect. Lace the front of the bodice with silk or cord to match its ground colour, or with green to tone with the skirt. Embroider tiny circles in buttonhole stitch round the point where the cord goes through the bodice, to simulate eyelet holes, in green or white cotton. Actual sewing cotton is better than embroidery silk for this purpose, being thinner and crisper in outline.

Make the only apron of white muslin, 4 in × 3 in, gathered at the waist on to a ribbon tie. Ornament the bottom with five lines of embroidery, two broad and three narrow, and use a light colour — blue, white or gold — for the broad bands. I used two bands of blue feather-stitch, outlined by three rows of pale gold stem stitch. (See Figure 37.)

The bonnet is cut from the pattern used for *Rosa*, but in black felt. Chain-stitch down the length of the front section, in gold embroidery silk, $\frac{1}{4}$ in from the front edge, and $\frac{1}{2}$ in from the back edge. Fill the gap with a double row of 'daisies', staggering the rows, as shown in Figure 40. Make two circles of chain-stitch on the back of the bonnet, $\frac{1}{2}$ in and $\frac{3}{4}$ in in from the edge, and fill the centre of the circle with daisies. Oversew the felt to join the two sections, and add narrow chin ties in blue ribbon.

Figure 40. Bonnet embroidery.
Cut pattern Fig. 38 in felt.

Finish her with white socks, black shoes, as for *Rosa*, and either blonde plaits, or short curly hair in simple style.

Gipsy Rosina (Plate 3)

Rosina has pantaloons and petticoat, cut 1 in shorter than for *Rosa*, and trimmed with red or black lace. Her chemise should be cut in thin muslin or nylon, and may be slightly transparent. Embroider the neck and sleeves in bright red. Her skirt is also 1 in shorter than *Rosa's*, in bright red or flaming orange. It is trimmed with four rows of black ric-rac braid, commencing $\frac{3}{4}$ in from the hem, or with three rows of black herringbone, if ric-rac is unobtainable.

Her bodice is cut from the pattern used for *Rosa*, altered at the front as shown in Figure 41. Make it in black nylon velvet, and chain-stitch in red round the neck, front and back edges, $\frac{1}{2}$ in in. Stitch a row of gold or silver sequins representing the coins worn on their

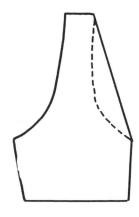

Figure 41. Bodice alteration, from Fig. 35.

44

persons by the gipsies for safe-keeping, down the front, between the edge and the line of red embroidery, letting them swing from a loop of thread, either in toning gold/silver, or in red. The sequins along the bottom and back should hang down just beyond the edge of the bodice.

The stockings can be in a bright colour — anything except red (or orange if the skirt is orange). The shoes are cut in felt, either in black, or in a bright colour. No aprons are worn — *Rosina* isn't a working girl.

The head is covered by the traditional gipsy scarf, made from a triangle of bright coloured material, not matching any of the colours used before in her costume. It can be patterned, as psychedelic as you wish, or plain and outlined with embroidery in several colours. Tie the ends behind the head, and let them hang down over her shoulder. The top front of the scarf should have a row of sequins stitched to it, and she wears earrings, either big sequins, or gold-coloured curtain rings, hanging down from her scarf at ear level. Her hair is black or dark brown, and dressed in a loose wavy style, shoulder-length or a little below. Her eyes are dark, and her expression lively.

She should carry a tambourine in one hand — stuck with glue, or secured to it by a pin. You may have a bottle top, or pill-box top which is just the right size, in bright plastic or cardboard. If not, cut one out in cardboard, according to the pattern in Figure 42. Stick a circle of coloured paper on the top, and a different colour around the sides, or paint them. Stick or sew a row of sequins around the side, as well. Ideally, they should hang down over the edge and move a little in the breeze. Stick or sew short lengths of bright ribbon or plaited wool to the edge in two places, making small bunches.

She can also have a hanging pocket, for the money she collects when she plays her tambourine. Make this from two scraps of felt, in a dark colour, one $1\frac{1}{2}$ in square, and the other $1\frac{1}{2}$ in $\times$ $2\frac{1}{4}$ in. Curve the bottom corners of both pieces, and the top corners of the larger piece. Starting a $\frac{1}{4}$ in inside the edge of the smaller piece, chain-stitch round and around, in a spiral, towards the centre of the piece, leaving an $\frac{1}{8}$ in gap between the lines. Use a bright colour, in embroidery silk or sewing cotton, then repeat the process with another bright colour, working your line in the gaps between the previous chains. I used red and peacock blue, on navy blue felt. Then stitch the two pieces together as indicated (Figure 43) with stabbing stitches, and chain-stitch on

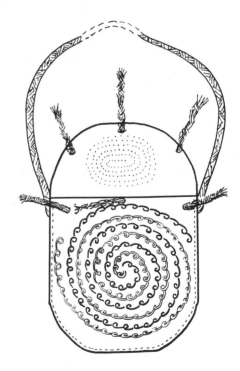

Figure 43. Money bag.
First decorate front with two different coloured spirals in chain-stitch, and flap with double oval, also back if wished. Stab stitch two sides together, and add plaited shoulder loop and ties.

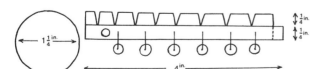

Figure 42. Tambourine.
Cut in stiff card, score down centre line, bend up tabs, and stick to underside of circle. Cover with adhesive plastic, and dangle sequins from edge on threads.

45

top of these, $\frac{1}{8}$ in from the edge. Turn over the projecting flap, and stitch a similar pattern in it, following the shape of the flap. If you feel really energetic, chain-stitch a double spiral on the back of the purse too, before you stitch the two sides together. Plait together three lengths of wool in different colours, about 7 in long from knot to knot at either end. Stitch the knots to either side of the purse, at the back of the flap, and make two similar short plaits of wool to tie the flap to the front of the bag. *Rosina* can carry the bag diagonally across her hip, or over one shoulder.

Hungarian Hattie (Plate 3)

Hattie wears her pantaloons and petticoat 1 in shorter than *Rosa*, and her chemise top is not turned over to make a frill. Instead, make a very small hem, and gather directly on the neckline. Embroider a line of feather-stitch over these gathers at the edge of the neck, in red, then make a single line of stitches $\frac{1}{8}$ in away, all round the neck. Now work a line of feather-stitch in blue, across the front of the chemise only, about $1\frac{1}{2}$ in long, the same distance below the line as above. Underline it in red, then in blue, with the same gap, and same length. Feather-stitch below this, in red, just less than 1 in long. Underline in blue, then red, and complete the front with a tiny line of blue feather-stitch, $\frac{1}{2}$ in long, underlined in red and blue, with a red dot at the very bottom of the triangle (see Figure 44). Make a double row

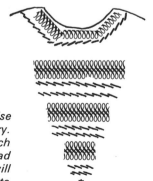

Figure 44. Chemise embroidery. Feather and stem stitch are shown, but any broad and narrow bands will substitute.

of red feather-stitching at the wrist of the sleeve, with no gap between, then copy the front pattern from top to bottom of the sleeve, keeping the length of the lines even all the way down, at about $\frac{1}{2}$ in or so. Don't fasten off your thread each time, but take it down to the next place where the colour is needed, to prevent lumps in the work. If you prefer, substitute a floral motif between the lines on the sleeve.

Make the skirt 1 in shorter than *Rosa's*, in a relatively subdued, but not drab, cotton. I used a soft bluish-pink. The under apron is black cotton, with a band of bright fabric across the bottom, starting $\frac{1}{2}$ in from the hem. This could be a strip patterned with flowers, or geometric designs, or may be plain, with flowers embroidered on top — with big, vulgar petals. This can be done in satin-stitch, or small pieces of coloured material can be appliquéd to the strip, in flower shapes. See Chapter Five for the stitches.

The short upper apron is only 2 in long, and can be made from a scrap of broderie anglaise, or textured muslin or nylon in white or a pale cream. Attach the two aprons to the same ribbon tie.

Cut the front bodice all in one piece, in felt, cutting the front $\frac{1}{2}$ in lower, to display the embroidery. Join one side and one shoulder only, and slip this on over one arm. Then oversew the other shoulder and side neatly together. Use felt for her boots, cut from pattern Figure 45. Make the boot leg and fit it on the doll's leg, then add the stuffed and stiffened toe section.

Hattie has two hats — one for a girl and one for a married lady. The girl wears a black felt pot hat, made from a circle of felt $2\frac{1}{4}$ in in diameter, and a strip 8 in × $1\frac{1}{2}$ in, oversewn together with the tiniest possible stitches. According to the tension of the sewing, there may be a minute surplus, which should be pared away at the top, but left at the bottom of the hat. Stitch the back seam, making it flat. There will be just a slight extra fullness at the bottom, which makes the hat sit better. Turn the hat, and attach half-a-dozen streamers of narrow ribbon or wool, to hang

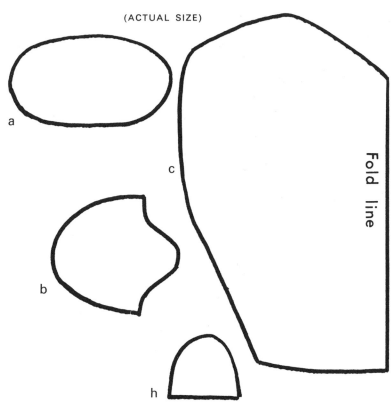

(ACTUAL SIZE)

a

c

b

h

Fold line

*Figure 45. Boots (basic).
Average size, adjust to leg as
stuffed. Make up and stiffen toe
section (a) and (b) as for shoes.
Stitch leg (c) to doll's leg, then
join at heel and instep. The
heel (h) is cut in cork $\frac{1}{4}$ in
high, painted or plastic faced
to match boot, and spiked to
sole.*

down past her shoulders. *Hattie* can have
brown or auburn plaits, or shoulder-length
curls, drawn back from her face.

If she married, *Hattie* would abandon her
pot hat and coloured streamers, and wear
white linen. Cut a strip $8\frac{3}{4}$ in × $2\frac{1}{2}$ in, and
make a $\frac{1}{2}$ in hem at the front long edge. This
can be machine-stitched, as it is covered
along the stitching line by two rows of chain-
stitch in red, close together. Make another
two rows along the back edge, beginning
$\frac{1}{2}$ in inside. Embroider or appliqué a line of
roses in the middle of this strip, covering an
area 3 in × $\frac{1}{2}$ in. Cut the back of the bonnet,
according to Figure 46 and, in blue, chain-
stitch three circles in the curved section,
starting $\frac{1}{2}$ in in from the raw edge. Embroider
a design of three roses and leaves, or appliqué
a flower cut from patterned cloth, in the centre
of this circle.

Now make up the bonnet back, matching
points X, Y and Z with those on the front
strip. Turn in all raw edges around the rest of

the back section, with a tiny hem. Pleat the
two ends of the front strip to fit the projecting
'ears' on the back section, and stitch firmly
into place. Place the bonnet on the head, and
fit it closely to the nape of the neck, securing
the hanging part of the back-cloth together
with a few stitches.

This cloth was intended to cover all *Mrs
Hattie's* hair, so it is not strictly necessary to
make a hairpiece at all. If you wish, give
her dark hair, tightly drawn back into a
single plait or roll, under the cloth, or let one
tiny ringlet escape at the front. Otherwise,
painted hair will suffice.

Olga the Bulgar (Plate 4)
Olga has pantaloons cut 1 in shorter than
Rosa's, and a petticoat, also 1 in shorter, and
1 in narrower from side to side, cut in fine
cotton. It is edged with a deep band of white
lace, as broad as you can find up to 1 in.
The bottom of her petticoat is embroidered

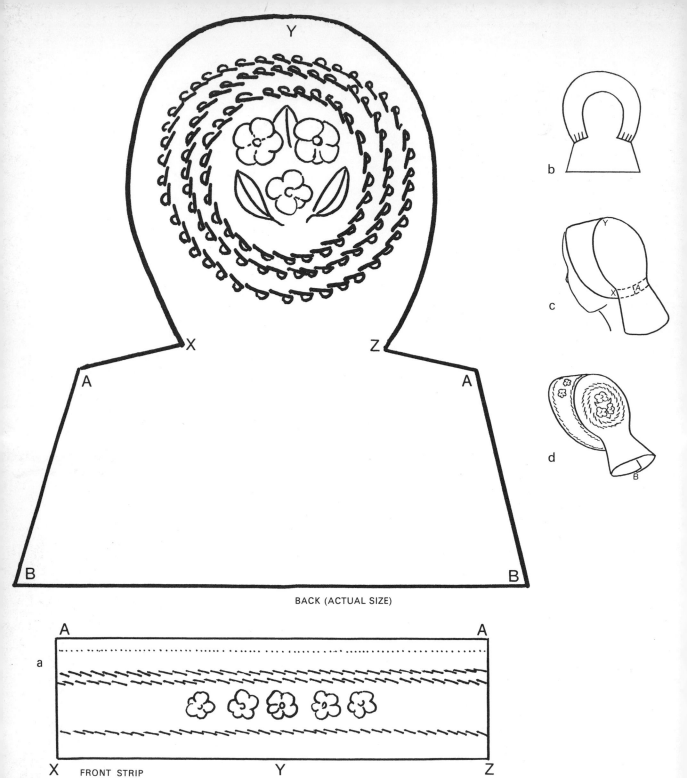

BACK (ACTUAL SIZE)

FRONT STRIP

Figure 46. Hungarian bonnet.
(a) Cut back from pattern and front strip to size given in text, in white cotton. Embroider or appliqué design. (b) Join front strip to back, gathering short side to fit. (c) Place on head, tucking lower projections under so that AA and BB meet. (d) Join and neaten AB.

Tamas, Olga
and Dick

George and
Martha Wash-
ington, and
English Rose

Henry VIII and Anne Boleyn

with thin chain-stitch lines and geometrical swirls to a depth of at least 1 in. I have drawn a possible pattern, but anything you may fancy along these lines will do, worked in red, green and blue (see Figure 47).

Figure 47. Olga's petticoat decoration.

Cut the chemise with sleeves just below the elbow, and edge the wrist with the same broad lace used for the petticoat. Gather the end of the sleeve and decorate with one line of chain-stitch in red, just above the lace trim. Work another line of red chain-stitch halfway along the upper arm, with a small geometric motif above it, occupying a space about 1 in square. Do not turn over a deep hem at the neck, or embroider all round with feather-stitch, but work a line of chain-stitch on top of the gathers, then make a 'bib' at the front, embroidering a floral spray, or a geometric pattern, in a triangular shape, $1\frac{1}{2}$ in wide at the top by about 1 in deep (Figure 48).

Cut the bodice front in one piece, making a low curve instead of a 'sweetheart' neckline (see Figure 49). Cut the back in two pieces, for ease in dressing the doll. Use black cotton or sateen, with a slightly shiny finish if possible. Edge the front neckline with green

ribbon or braid, then with red braid $\frac{1}{2}$ in inside the neckline. Dress the doll, and stitch the back opening.

Cut the skirt in the same black material, but 1 in narrower all round than the pattern for *Rosa*, and just below knee length, so that, when the doll is dressed, all the petticoat embroidery will show. The skirt can be stitched to the bodice edge. Decorate the bottom of the skirt with a band of green braid, $\frac{1}{2}$ in from the bottom, and make an appliquéd, geometric pattern in red braid and green embroidery above it, at least 1 in wide. A suggested pattern is given in Figure 50, but make up your own if you wish. The only principle is that this should be rich, fat embroidery, while that on the petticoat is thin and spiky.

Figure 50. Olga's over-skirt embroidery.

Olga should have a silver belt, which can be made of silver ribbon, preferably textured, or narrow silver foil. Close the belt with a 'buckle' — either a button in silver, or an old metal brooch which has lost its stones. She can also have a silver button at her throat.

Her hair is black, in two plaits, or drawn back from the head, secured at the back of the head with a twist of gold wire, decorated with sequins, and plaited in about a dozen tiny plaits (Figure 51). These are fixed at the

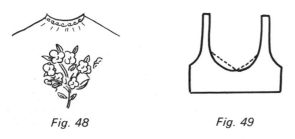

Fig. 48   Fig. 49

Figure 48. Olga's chemise embroidery.
Figure 49. Olga's bodice alteration to Figure 35.

Figure 51. Olga's hair, rear view. Attach long strands, in any number divisible by three, and bind with gold bar at upper shoulder level. Make six or twelve thin plaits below this, and join all tails in thick centre plait. Tie with coloured wool and gold wire.

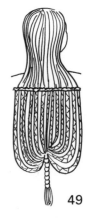

bottom to a piece of gold wire, with a bobble or tassel on the end. Fuse wire will do admirably, though Christmas goodies sometimes have little bits of gold wound wire in their wrappings.

She wears sandals, so make up only the toe and sole section of the shoe pattern, in light coloured felt, and secure them to the foot with a strip around the ankle, down the back and across the instep (Figure 52).

*Figure 52. Sandals.
Use shoe pattern, Figure 39 a and b only, with felt or ribbon straps round heel and ankle.*

Hendrikje from Holland (Plate 1)

In Holland, the North Sea wind blows every day, without ceasing, so the trees grow at an angle of 45° to the ground, and the women wear seven petticoats. This is a bit much for a doll, but our *Hendrikje* has four, though we will cheat a little by making two of them shorter, and join them below the waistline. Cut two petticoats in thin cotton, one 4 in long, the other 5 in, and slimmer by 1 in than the normal size. Cut two more thin petticoats full length. Hem all the bottom edges, and align the four. Stitch petticoat A to petticoat B where they meet, and petticoat B to petticoat C as shown. Join C and D at the waist, and anchor the whole lot to the waist of the doll (Figure 53).

*Figure 53. Dutch petticoats.
Align bottom edges of all petticoats and stitch (a) and (b) to the next petticoat where they meet it.*

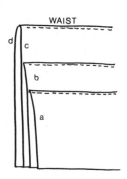

It is too cold to wear a light chemise and sleeveless bodice, so Dutch girls cover themselves with a short-sleeved chemise and

(ACTUAL SIZE)

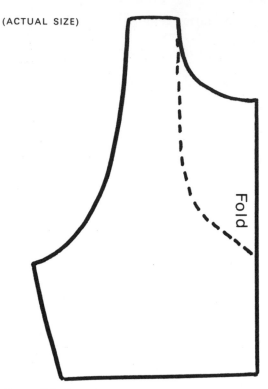

*Figure 54. Hendrikje's bodice front.
Use Figure 35 a for back, cut in two sections instead of on fold.*

a long-sleeved woollen bodice. Make a chemise in the finest possible fabric, without sleeves, and not embroidered, or omit the garment altogether, since it will not be seen, if no thin muslin is available. Alter the front bodice pattern to give a higher, round neck (Figure 54) and cut in one piece. Cut the back of the bodice in two pieces, for ease in dressing. Make a slimmer sleeve pattern (Figure 55) cut to elbow length. When made up, turn the elbow end over in a deep cuff, trimmed with 'apron' fabric (see below). Finish the neck of the bodice with a simple, small hem. Make up the garment and put on from the front, securing the back seam later. To make up for the visible chemise top, *Hendrikje* wears a lace bib front (Fig 56) in broad lace, broderie anglaise, or made of several thinner strips basted together. Edge with a narrow lace frill.

Her skirt is in a rich, dark colour — using any colour not used for the bodice. No apron

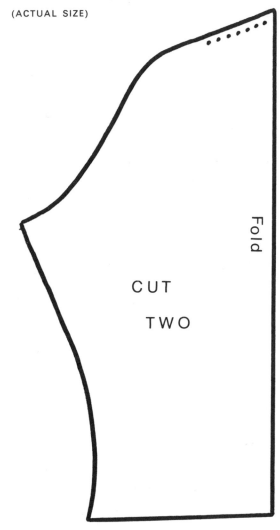

Fold

CUT

TWO

Figure 55. Bodice sleeves.

Figure 56. Bib front.
Cut from a single piece of coarse white lace or broderie anglaise, or build up from strips of narrow lace. Edge with narrow lace, lightly gathered.

in the ordinary sense was worn, but a band of fabric at the top of the skirt, right around the hips. Use either a material patterned in bands, with the ground colour matching the skirt, such as a strip of striped and figured curtain material, or toning check fabric. Trim the sleeves with the same fabric at the cuff.

She should have striped stockings, in blue/white or red/white, or a heavily patterned rib, and, of course, clogs. These are undoubtedly best carved in balsa wood, hardwood or cork, but can be moulded from Plasticine, and laminated in papier mâché, or cast in plaster or epoxy resin. The shape need not be hollowed out fully, since the doll's foot does not project into the toe cavity.

Holland has a greater variety of headgear than almost any other country, with different shapes and sizes for each town, province, age and social group, and also variations for marital status and religion. The well-known Dutch bonnet style is the Vollendam winged cap, and I have given instructions for making this, and a prettier Zeeland bonnet.

The winged cap is often made in white lace, which is starched into position, with the wings of the cap turned up by the cheeks. It is quite difficult to get an even curve on both sides. If you want to attempt this, cut one pair of pieces from the pattern, Figure 57, in coarse white lace, and baste them as invisibly as possible together. Line the wings with two triangular pieces of lace, cut from Figure 58, and edge the whole cap with narrow white lace. Make a skullcap of white or gold cotton (Figure 38) and stitch the bonnet to the skullcap, using the lace edging to disguise the join. Now starch the whole bonnet, pinning the lace wings into place till it dries, and pinning the top out stiffly, so that it does not collapse onto the skullcap.

A firmer cap can be made if the lace is fully lined with cotton, using the patterns in Figures 57 and 58, and the wing is then covered with the lace triangle as well. A still stronger cap is made if the whole thing is cut in cotton, outside and lining. Stitch the

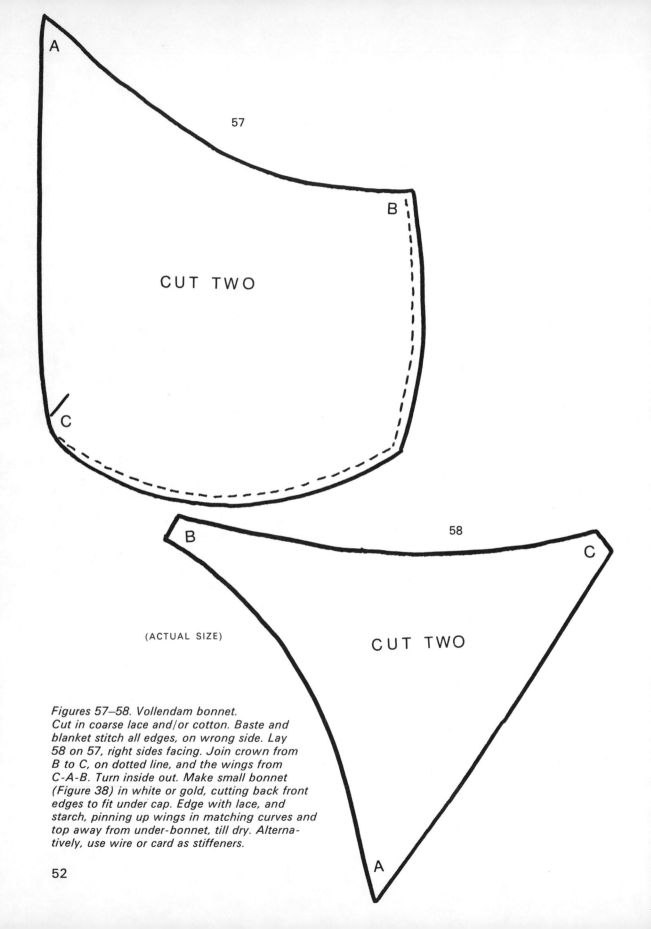

57

A

B

C

CUT TWO

58

B

C

(ACTUAL SIZE)

CUT TWO

A

Figures 57–58. Vollendam bonnet.
Cut in coarse lace and/or cotton. Baste and
blanket stitch all edges, on wrong side. Lay
58 on 57, right sides facing. Join crown from
B to C, on dotted line, and the wings from
C-A-B. Turn inside out. Make small bonnet
(Figure 38) in white or gold, cutting back front
edges to fit under cap. Edge with lace, and
starch, pinning up wings in matching curves and
top away from under-bonnet, till dry. Alterna-
tively, use wire or card as stiffeners.

outside pieces together, attach the wing linings, and the head lining at the front only. Turn to the right side, and either close the back, edge with lace, and starch, or stiffen the whole cap before you close the back with pieces of cardboard, cut from the lining patterns, and then trimmed smaller all round to fit. They can be inserted through the gap, and then stitched into place.

The Zeeland cap is more complicated to look at, but easier to make. There are several layers, of which the least visible is the hair. Only one small roll of hair, like a curled-under fringe, can be seen at the centre front. This is topped by a blue skullcap, but, as this is completely invisible in wear, you may prefer to omit it. Next comes a gold cap, fitting tightly over the hair, and outlining the face. Cut this as a bonnet, from the pattern in Figure 38. Stitch the two sections together, making a tiny hem at the front and neck edges. Cover this gold bonnet with a second, made of lace, either cut from a piece of wide lace to the same pattern, or made of edging lace, stitched round and round over the gold

bonnet, though only occasionally attached to it. The front edge must be free of stitching (see Figure 59). Now attach to the front edge of the gold cap, on either side of the fringe of hair, two little corkscrews of gold wire. These are often available as tiny lengths of spring, in some toys and electrical appliances, which break into short lengths, ideal for the purpose. Otherwise, gold wire or fuse wire, twisted into a corkscrew shape, is fine, about $\frac{1}{2}$ in–1 in long. Each pair of corkscrews should protrude forwards, like the horns of a charging bull.

For the superstructure, you will need a length of extravagantly patterned lace, 3 in wide by 14 in long. Old petticoats, particularly the bouffant half-slips of the late 'fifties, have this kind of trimming, or a strip from the bottom of a lace curtain may do. If it is not already stiffened, starch it at this stage, or insert thin gold wire around the edge. Cut a back section (Figure 60) and attach the frill to it, making a deep box pleat at the top (Figure 61). When the hat is in position, the join of the material should be where the

Figure 59. Zeeland cap. Attach wire spirals by stitching to under-bonnet, or spiking to head. Make under bonnet from Figure 38, curving front edge and gathering to fit head closely. Lace bonnet, to same pattern, fits closely at the bottom, but is left loose on top of the head.

Figure 60. Zeeland bonnet back pattern. Cut this and front strip (3 in × 14 in) in lace and starch before making up.

(ACTUAL SIZE)

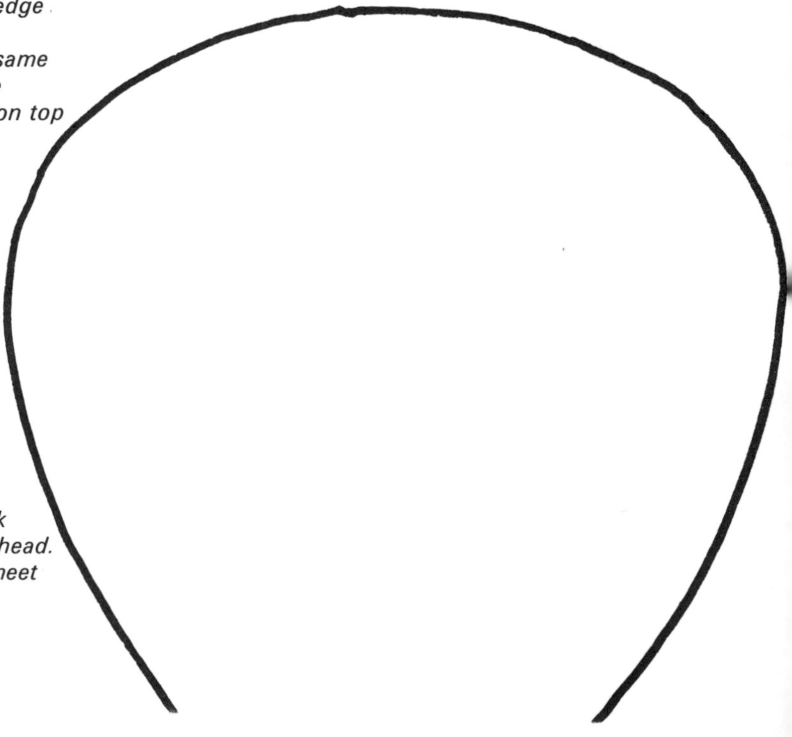

INSIDE

Figure 61. Attach front to back with deep box pleat at top of head. Curve front lower corners to meet back, or turn over and tack in place.

natural hair crown would be. Tack down here, and about 1 in further forward, to fix the inside of the pleat to the lace cap. The front of the frill should stand out around the face, with a heart-shaped curve over the head (Figure 62). Tack the side front of the

Figure 62. Front view. Form top into heart-shaped curve, stiffening edge with wire if necessary. Trim with narrow lace or muslin frill.

bonnet to the inner lace cap, at the bottom, to steady it, and stitch a small lace bow and streamers to the back neck edge. Two lace ties may be added to the front, to go under the chin.

If you have a small coral necklace, this could be wound several times round the neck (in which case, you can omit the lace ties). A metal button or stoneless brooch may be added at the front below the lace bib.

Long plaits go with the winged cap, but the Zeeland cap is meant to cover all the hair except the little fringe. *Hendrikje* has a healthy colour, from the wind, with rosy cheeks and blue eyes.

English Rose (Plate 5)

Oddly enough, there is no very definite English 'national' costume for women, perhaps because of the early impact of the Industrial Revolution. England never had a static 'peasant class' and remote aristocracy. *Rose*, at Manor Farm, wore the same clothes as *Miss Charlotte* at the Manor, though perhaps in cheaper fabrics. The style I have chosen is one which had a long run in the 1760s and 1770s, then came back again in the early 1800s, because it was so pretty. It is thought of as 'milkmaid', because so many artists have painted milkmaids wearing it, though ladies wore it too.

Rose wears unhistorical pantaloons, just below the knee, and a white petticoat to the ankle. She also has a sleeveless chemise top, in white muslin, gathered at the neck, and edged with narrow lace. The gathers were made by slotting ribbon through the cloth, and this can best be simulated by making tacking stitches in blue, black or green thick embroidery silk or cord, and finishing with a bow, in front under the lace frill.

Her second petticoat, or underdress, is exposed to view, and can be cut in either a small floral print, or in striped cotton, with vertical stripes. Both petticoats should be gathered, and have most of the fullness pushed to the side in bunches, with a little at the back, and a flat front.

The bodice is close fitting, with elbow-length sleeves, edged with a frill of muslin, 1 in deep, with pinked or selvage edge, and has a stomacher point, which comes below the waist. Cut the bodice from the patterns in Figure 63 a–c, in a plain cotton toning with one of the colours in the flowered underdress, or in a sprigged or textured cloth, to go with stripes. Stitch the points of the stomacher down to the underdress. The top of the bodice should reveal the frill and ribbon of the chemise.

Cut a strip, 11 in × 4 in, in the same fabric as the bodice, and tiny hem the top and sides. Turn a deeper hem at the bottom, but do not press the edge flat, so that there is a kind of roll here. Gather the top to fit the waistline, then gather the two ends of the strip as tightly as possible. Anchor the gathers with a second line of stitches, and turn the gathered edge underneath, so that a loose bunch of fabric is left. This bunch sits at the front of the hip, and a second line of looser gathers is made vertically at the back of the hip on each side. This overskirt therefore has two deep puffs of fabric over each hip, and a lesser puff over the bottom. Rich ladies wore boomerang-shaped padded cushions under their skirt, to hold out this 'pannier' style skirt (Figure 64).

Rose covers her neckline lightly with a semi-transparent loose scarf of thin muslin

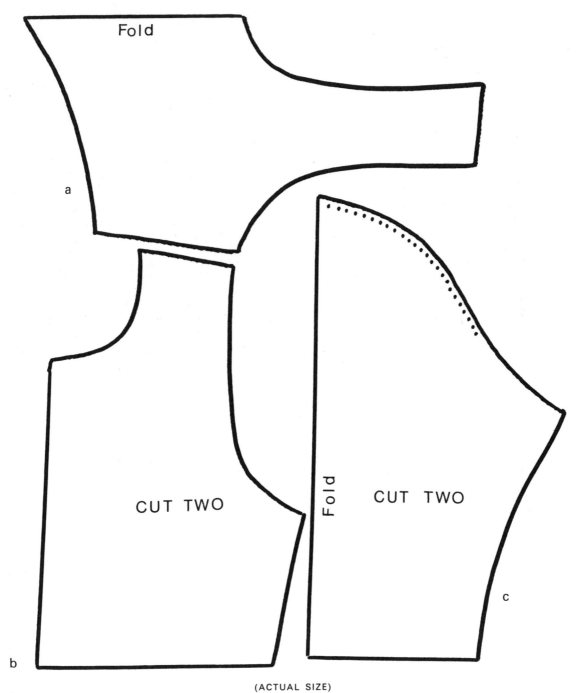

Fold

a

b

CUT TWO

Fold

CUT TWO

c

(ACTUAL SIZE)

Figure 63.
Rose's bodice. (a) Front. (b) Back. (c) Sleeve.

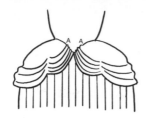

Figure 65. Fichu.
Gather ends of muslin strip 11 in × 2½ in and
baste invisibly to centre front of bodice. Drape,
and baste at back and shoulder if necessary.

Figure 64. Pannier over-skirt.
Pleat ends of hemmed 11 in × 4 in strip tightly.
Gather tightly at front and less tightly at
back to make bunches of fabric over hips and
rear, as shown. Gather top of strip to fit waist
from A-A. Attach pleated ends to sides of
stomacher point.

or gauze, attached to her bodice at the centre front, and draped round her shoulders. Cut as Figure 65, and invisibly tack in position.

Her head is covered by a mob cap, made of a circle of white thin cotton, trimmed with a pinked muslin frill or gathered lace, and gathered by a ribbon of embroidery cord, with a bow in front. Cut a circle 6 in in diameter, if lace edging is to be used, or 7 in if it is to be pinked, and gather to leave a ½ in frill. This cap sits high on hair in a warm brown, dressed in curls and ringlets, reaching halfway down the shoulder. Crêpe hair is much the best for this.

CHAPTER 7

Tamas, Dick and Hans

Because they went out into the world more, mixing with the rich, as masters or traders, peasant men were far more fashion-conscious, and varied in their styles of dress. The women had one basic wide skirt, but the men wore breeches, long wide trousers, long tight trousers, or shorts. Over their shirts, they wore waistcoats, jackets, jerkins, blouses, long coats or cloaks. Only their headgear was less elaborate and varied. However, if you have made a set of girl dolls in traditional dress, then you may wish to pair them off with their menfolk.

These can all be made on the *Rag Rosy* body, with front stuffing adjusted to suit, or on the *Cloth Charles*. He is taller and more shapely, which may be an advantage in displaying shorts or tight trousers. Also, since he is wired, it is easier to pose him for action, or give him something to carry.

Hans (Plate 2)

Hans will escort the basic *Rosa*, or the *Tyrolean Mädchen*. He is a mountaineer, so he wears shorts, for scrambling over rocks, or chasing wayward cattle and tourists. These are Lederhosen — made of leather, in fact — and you may have suitable material from an old pair of gloves, or a piece of chamois leather. If the leather is water-stained, this will add to the realism. Lederhosen were worn and never washed, till they grew strong enough to walk away from their owner. Handbag leather, or plastic, may do as a substitute, though handbags are usually too thick, and plastic too thin, to work without difficulty. The one splits, and the other makes

your fingers ache with the effort of stitching. The colour should be buff, pale fawn or pale gray, and the surface matt rather than shiny. The seams can be stab stitched on the edge, if the projection is very small, overlapped and stitched flat, to simulate topstitching, or joined with tiny cross-stitches, according to the thickness of the leather. See the Chapter Five on stitches.

Hans should first be dressed in drawers, cut from the pantaloon pattern (Figure 32), and shortened to match the Lederhosen. If you have some old-fashioned, rough cream underwear which Grandpa used to wear, this is ideal, or use beige cotton. Then cut out the Lederhosen pattern pieces, Figure 66 a–b. Join all seams except the outer side seam above pocket level P. Decorate the bottom of the leg with black cross-stitch for the last inch, and form a bow with the ends of the embroidery cotton (Figure 67).

The front of the shorts should also be decorated. If your leather is thin enough to stitch without too much difficulty, this can be done by embroidery. If not, mark the design in felt-tip pens or paint, using green, gold and black (Figure 68). Outline the edge of the pocket with green braid, embroidery, or felt-tip pen. Now fit the shorts, and lap the front edge over the pocket projections, and stitch in place.

The shirt is in white, cut from the patterns in Figure 69 a–c. The back is cut in two pieces, for convenience in dressing. Join the side and shoulder seams, make up, and insert sleeves as for chemise. Hem and gather wrists to fit loosely. Make up collar pieces as shown (Figure 70) and attach at neck.

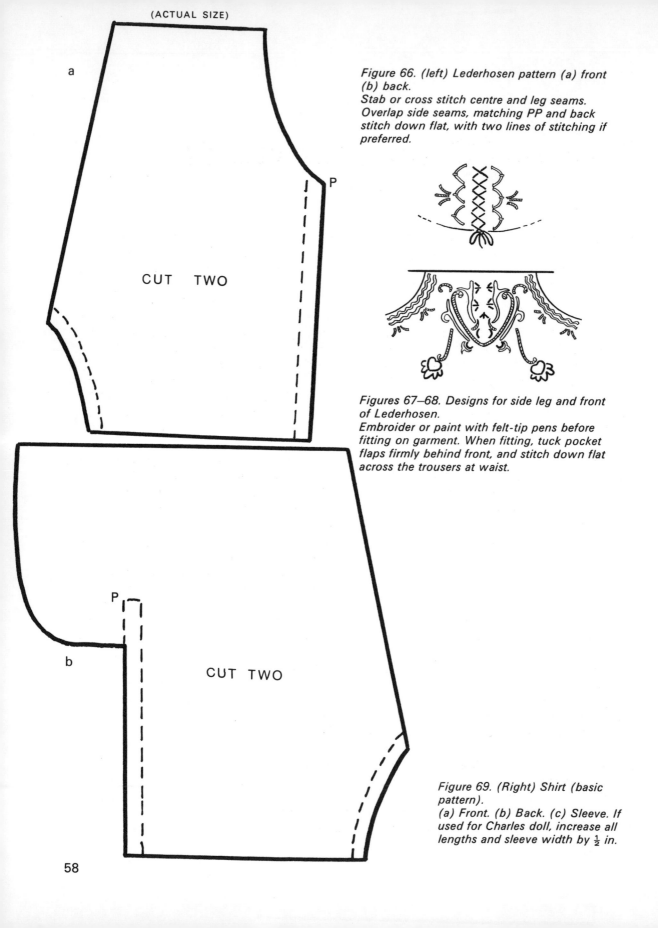

(ACTUAL SIZE)

a

CUT TWO

P

Figure 66. (left) Lederhosen pattern (a) front (b) back.
Stab or cross stitch centre and leg seams. Overlap side seams, matching PP and back stitch down flat, with two lines of stitching if preferred.

Figures 67–68. Designs for side leg and front of Lederhosen.
Embroider or paint with felt-tip pens before fitting on garment. When fitting, tuck pocket flaps firmly behind front, and stitch down flat across the trousers at waist.

P

b

CUT TWO

Figure 69. (Right) Shirt (basic pattern).
(a) Front. (b) Back. (c) Sleeve. If used for Charles doll, increase all lengths and sleeve width by $\frac{1}{2}$ in.

58

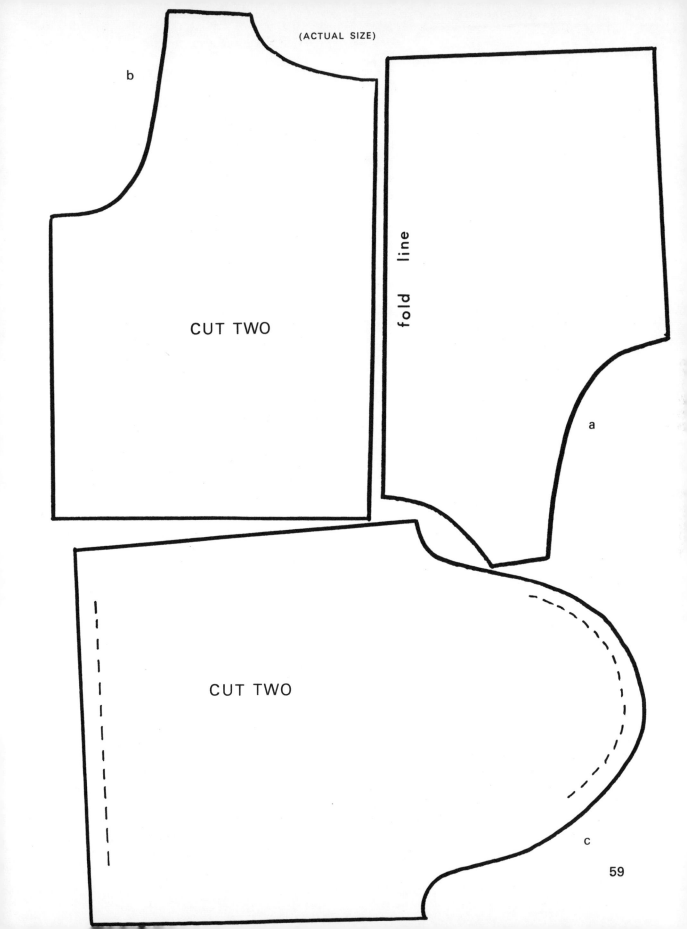

(ACTUAL SIZE)

b

CUT TWO

fold line

a

CUT TWO

c

59

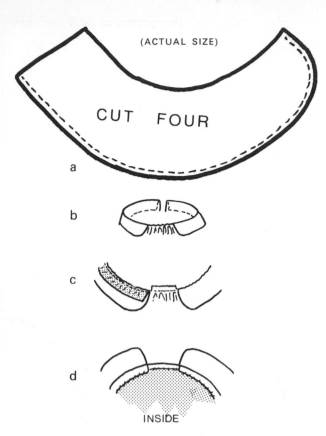

(ACTUAL SIZE)

CUT FOUR

a

b

c

d

INSIDE

Figure 70. (a) Shirt collar pattern.
For front gathered shirt, make up in two sections,
turn, and lay against neck edge of shirt,
with flat end of collar to centre back of neck
(b) Sandwich collars between shirt front and
bias strip; machine together (c), turn to inside,
and hem invisibly the bias strip, and the small
gap at the front of neck (d).

Figure 71. Belt and braces, embroidered on
coloured tape.

Attach a bow of red ribbon at the neck, with the ends dangling down, not sticking out sideways.

Trousers are held up by a belt and braces, both bright and embroidered, in rich colours. Coloured cotton tape, feather-stitched down the middle, with either chain-stitch or a zigzag stitch on the edge, in white on red, yellow on blue, or any colour except green would look well (Figure 71). The belt should be broader than the braces – double the tape – and fastened with a silver buckle, or square brooch or button. Silver foil on card will do.

The next garment is a waistcoat, cut from the patterns in Figure 72 a and b. It should be green, cut either in felt or cloth, adding $\frac{1}{4}$ in for turnings if cloth is used. The whole right front is edged with silver or gold buttons (or black ones), and the left front with simulated button-holes, made of short lengths of thick embroidery cord, oversewn into place as indicated, or worked in minute buttonhole-stitch, if you are neat. But do not cut a hole, even for the only two buttons which actually meet. Stitch these two on the buttonhole side, after lapping the fronts as indicated.

Hans also has a jacket, cut from the patterns in Figure 73 a–d. This is in buff, fawn or gray felt or cloth, to tone as nearly as possible with his trousers. Allow an extra $\frac{1}{4}$ in for turnings, if cloth is used. Make up the front, back and sleeves, in the usual way, and bind the wrists and edge of the jacket with green braid. Make the binding of the neck edge broader, by doubling the braid. Make button-holes – simulated or opening – down the left front, and stitch buttons on the right front. These should be the kind made of (apparently) plaited leather, which can sometimes be obtained pale, and dyed green. Ordinary dark brown or black ones would do, or plain green buttons in a small size.

Hans wears wool socks, in a fairly coarse rib, in white, fawn or pale gray, with coloured patterns embroidered down them, in green again. His boots are ankle-length, cut from the same cow as were his shorts, if you have enough leather left, or from fawn or gray felt.

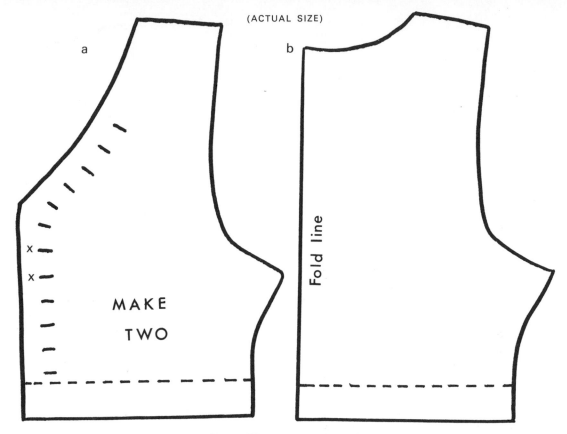

Figure 72. Waistcoat (basic).
(a) Back, (b) Front. Cut on dotted lines for felt, unless Charles model is used. Make holes, in button-hole stitch or cord, down left front, and buttons, with sequins or spirals of gold or silver wire, down right front as marked. Overlap sides at XX only, and stitch two buttons on top of holes at this point.

Cut the boots from the pattern in Figure 74 a–c, and let the stitching on the seams show aggressively, with extra lines across the toecap, and the heel. Add black or green 'shoe laces' with a bow.

Hans should be made up tanned, knees as well as face, and have a little moustache, slightly wider than the brush style. His hair is relatively short, and can be stitched on with no hanging ends (Figure 18), or made in a close-fitting wig. His hair can be blond, or a bright brown. His hat has a brim and tallish crown, cut in brown felt as Figure 75 a–c with the edge of the brim, as marked, stitched inside the crown of the hat. He has a bunch of five or six white or coloured feathers at the front of his hat.

He should be doing something — carrying a coil of rope (string) to rescue someone from the mountains, or an ice axe, or a Stein beer mug.

Gipsy Pedro (Plate 3)
Although *Rosina* wears a central European costume, the male gipsy is usually represented in a somewhat Spanish outfit. He wears a chemise-patterned shirt, gathered high to the neck, then slit open in the centre for 1 in (Figure 76), with narrow red embroidery at the neck and gathered wrists.

Over this, he wears a bolero waistcoat, cut from pattern Figures 72 a and 77, in a bright colour — red, purple, peacock blue, in thin velvet or a shiny material. Trim the whole edge with braid or ribbon in a contrasting colour, say emerald green on red, or attach gold or silver sequins down the front and

Figure 73. Jacket (basic).
(a) Back. (b) Front. (c) Sleeve. Increase
length for Charles model. (d) Cut collar from
bias strip, fold over on line, stitch ends, turn
and attach to neck edge. This collar stands up-
right when finished.

a

Fo

(ACTUAL SIZE)

b

F
o
l
d

C U T

C U T   T W O

← 1 in. →

$6\frac{3}{4}$ in.

c

d

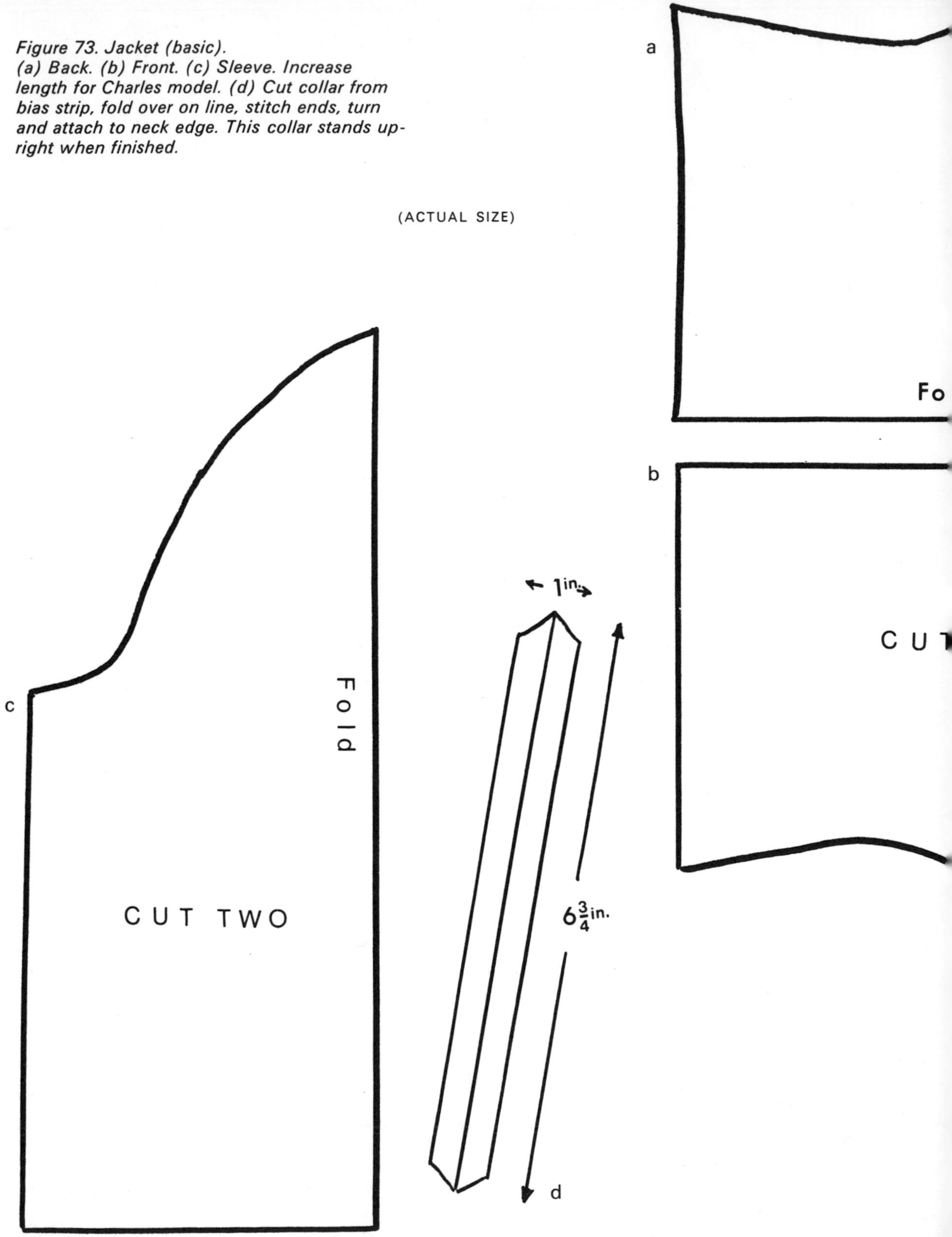

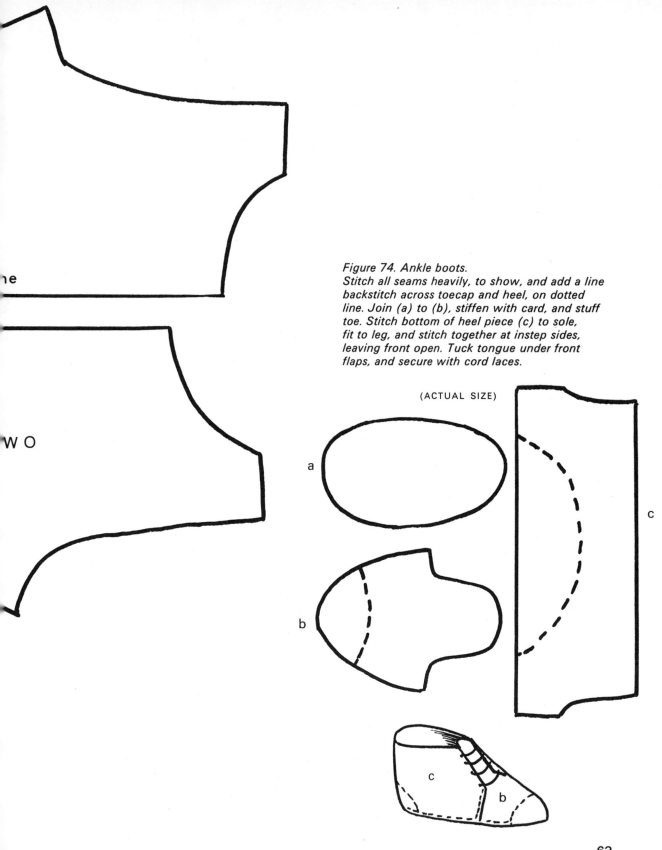

ne

W O

Figure 74. Ankle boots.
Stitch all seams heavily, to show, and add a line
backstitch across toecap and heel, on dotted
line. Join (a) to (b), stiffen with card, and stuff
toe. Stitch bottom of heel piece (c) to sole,
fit to leg, and stitch together at instep sides,
leaving front open. Tuck tongue under front
flaps, and secure with cord laces.

(ACTUAL SIZE)

a

b

c

c

b

63

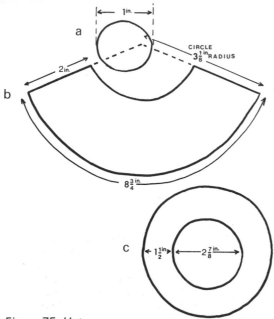

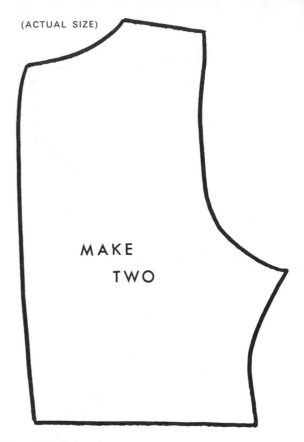

(ACTUAL SIZE)

MAKE

TWO

Figure 75. Hat.
Oversew or cross-stitch (a) to (b). Place edge
of crown (b) over inner edge of brim (c), and
backstitch into position. Add a bunch of
feathers near front.

Figure 76. Pedro's shirt
neck detail.
Use pattern Figure 34
for shirt.

Figure 77. Bolero front.
Use Figure 72 a for back.

along the outer edges, as for *Rosina*, so
that they swing free.

As far as I know, *Pedro* does not wear
underpants at all, so go straight on to the
trousers, which are long and tight-fitting.
Make them green to match the bolero braid,
or whatever colour you used. The material
can be glazed cotton or sateen, with a shine
to it. Cut from pattern Figure 78, adjusted
as necessary. Join the leg and front seams,
and dart to shape. Then embroider a curving
design to outline where *Pedro* would have a
pocket, if he allowed such a thing to spoil
the line of the trousers. Use black thread,
also for a design down the side of the trouser
leg (Figure 79), inside which are sequins
in line. Put the trousers on him, tighten the
darts, and stitch back to fit tightly. Add a
cummerbund of bright material, say bright

blue, around the waist, pulled tight, with a
scarf knot and tails hanging to the knee.

Pedro's skin is swarthy, his eyes black, and
his hair black and shortish, but curly. His headgear is a scarf like *Rosina's*, in bright
material, but without the line of sequins. He
wears large earrings and a gold chain around
his neck. His feet are sockless, and his shoes
are black.

In his hand, *Pedro* carries a violin, to
accompany *Rosina's* tambourine playing.
This can be cut to shape (Figure 80) from
three pieces of cardboard. Two are stuck
together complete, and the third slotted to
form a recess in which the finger-board is
stuck. This can be made of a piece of wood,
flat on one face, and curved on the other — a
split pencil of small enough size will do
admirably. Add a scrap of wood at the other

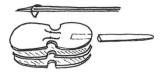

Figure 80. Violin detail.

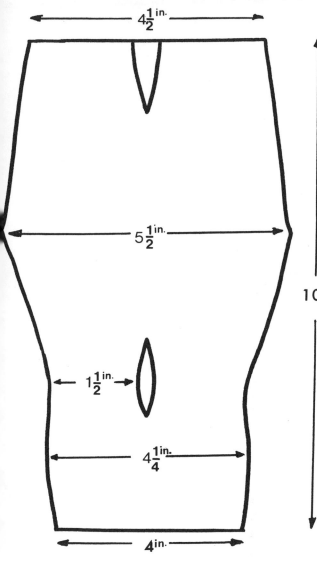

Figure 78. Trousers (basic).
Draw out to given dimensions on card, adjusting length for individual dolls. They are meant to fit very closely, so stitch dart loosely on wrong side, leaving thread, and pull it tight when the garment is fitted.

Figure 79. Trousers decoration.
Do this before final fitting on.

end, a tiny piece of card to make a bridge, and use fuse wire to make the strings. The curved head of the finger-board, with the pegs, will have to be carved in wood, moulded in papier mâché pulp, or shaped in wire and covered with black adhesive plastic. In his other hand he holds a bow, made of an orange stick or cocktail stick, with a twist of wire to hold the gut, made of embroidery silk. In case his playing does not please, he has a short knife of cardboard in his belt. Both the fingerboard and knife-handle should be black, the body of the violin brown, and the knife blade silver. Draw the S-shaped holes and the finger-board markings for the violin in felt-tip pen.

Hungarian Ladislas (Plate 2)
Ladislas wears a chemise-cut shirt (Figure 34), gathered at the neck, but with the sleeves loose, and edged with broderie anglaise, or a pinked frill. His shirt hangs outside his trousers. The neck has a stand-up band of tape or cotton, to form a collar, and under the collar is a tie, made from dark blue ribbon, 6 in long, edged with green braid in a lozenge shape (Figure 81), on which a cross is embroidered in gold, for the Hungarians are very religious.

Figure 81. Tie.

His trousers are knee-length breeches (Figures 82 a and b). Cut in grosgrain, or fine corduroy with the stripes running horizontally, in darkish blue or green. Decorate the trousers down the front with a motif

a

b

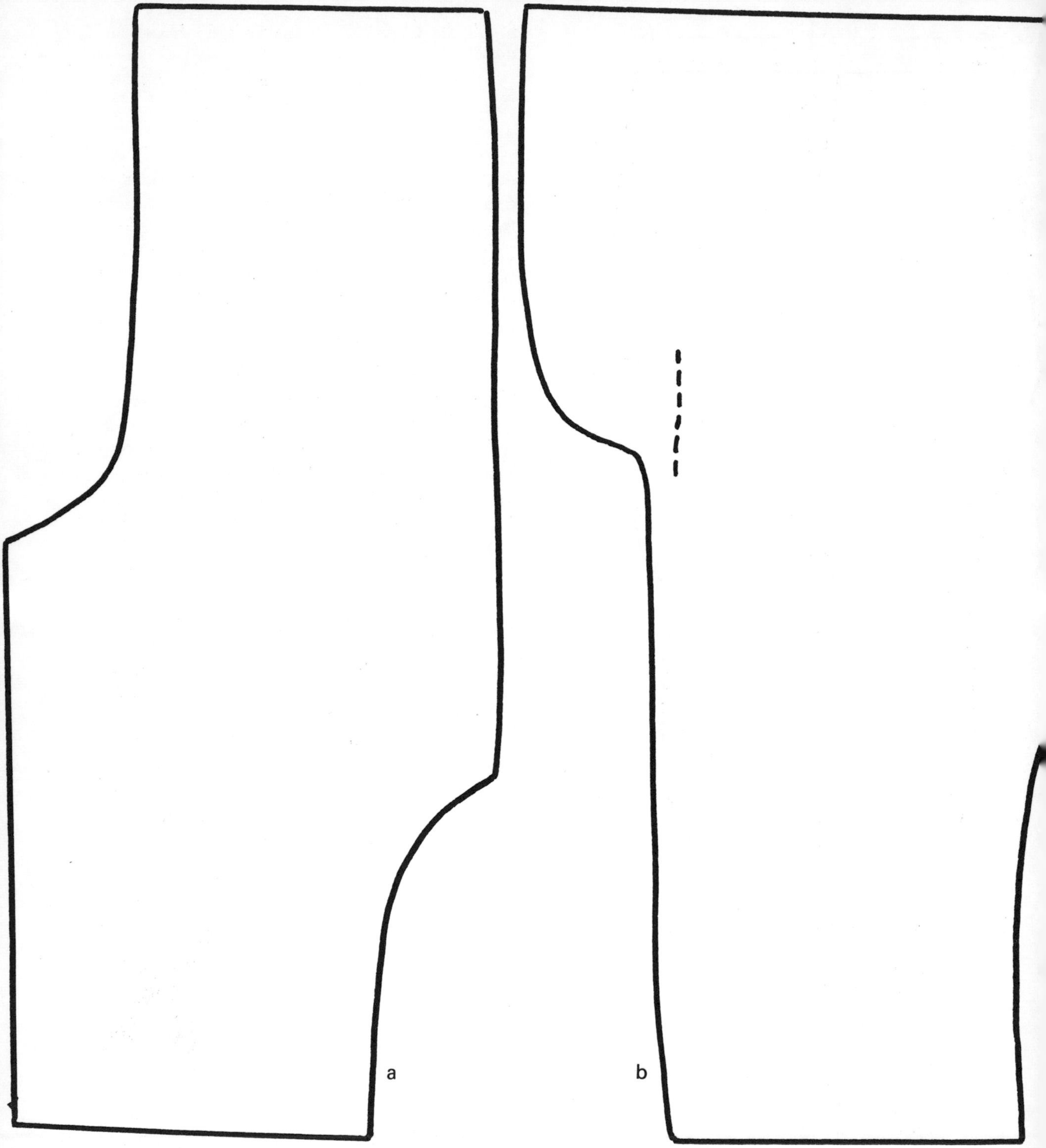

Figure 82 a (front), b (back). Breeches (basic).
Make up as for Lederhosen (Figure 66). Gather back of waist to fit closely.

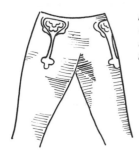

Figure 83. Breeches decoration.
Braid or embroider before final fitting.

ending in a cross, stitched in red and gold embroidery silk (Figure 83). As usual, make up the leg and front seams, and join the back neatly when the breeches are on the doll.

Ladislas wears white socks, in cotton rib, and black boots (Figure 45) with a curved top. Fit the boot leg on to the doll first, and join the stuffed foot on later. Add a gold tassel to the top of the boot. They may be found on chocolate boxes, or made of fuse wire.

Ladislas's great pride is his cloak, made of thick-looking, light-coloured cloth — buff, cream, pale green, say — cut as shown in Figures 84 a–c. Make the main cloak, join on the big lapel, which also forms a shawl collar. Edge this lapel with blue braid (or green, if the trousers are green). Cut small strips of red leather, plastic or thin felt, and appliqué them to the upper lapel in a ladder (Figure 85), and embroider two symbolic flowers below, in green and blue. Chain-stitch down the edge of the lapel, inside the braid, and add another symbolic flower at the bottom corner. The cloak is held in place by a $\frac{1}{2}$ in bar across the chest, made of the same material.

His hat is of black felt, with a low, pot-shaped crown and wide brim. Cut it as in Figure 86, and decorate it with a sprig of flowers, made of wire and paper.

Bulgarian Tamas (Plate 4)

Tamas wears a mid-blue shirt, cut like *Hans's*, but the sleeves are not gathered at the wrist. They are edged with three narrow bands of embroidery, similar in style to that on *Olga's* petticoat. He also has two lines of chain-stitch down his front, with a double row of small geometric shapes between them (Figure 87). They match the motif on *Olga's* sleeve. Use a single colour, red or green, for all the embroidery.

Tamas's trousers are long and tight, like *Pedro's*, but in a light colour — cream, light green, pink or light blue — with an embroidered motif on the upper thigh, as shown in Figure 88. From his knees down, his legs are cross-gartered, in a bright-coloured ribbon. Attach this ribbon at the knee, cross over down the leg, and attach the ends to his shoes, which are sandals, like *Olga's*. There will be a small gap between trousers and sandal, which can be filled by thin, coloured stockings, or a scrap of bright felt, set in the gap of the sandal.

He has a coat, cut from *Hans's* jacket pattern, but $\frac{1}{2}$ in longer, and flared out at the hem, as shown in Figure 89. Give him a stand-up collar in the same fabric, felt or firm cloth in deep green, maroon, rust-red, etc. Trim the bottom with contrasting braid, and stitch together at the neck only, to show off the shirt underneath.

His cap is cut from matching felt, two pieces as in Figure 90, joined, turned and edged with the same braid which trimmed his jacket. The sticking-up piece is at the back of the cap.

His hair is dark, and fits closely to the head. If made in wool or cotton, stitch the ends through the head, and do not leave loose pieces dangling.

He carries a flail, which can be shaped from wood, as in Figure 91a, or cut flat from a candy stick, or a bent twig with a milk can on it. Make this in cardboard as shown in Figure 91b, or from a slim bottle cap, adding a thread or wire handle.

Dutch Dirk (Plate 1)

Dirk also protects himself against that strong wind by layers of clothing. He wears thick underpants, of cream wool, or stockinet, cut to the pantaloon pattern. His shirt is cotton, cut like *Hans's*, without the stand-up collar,

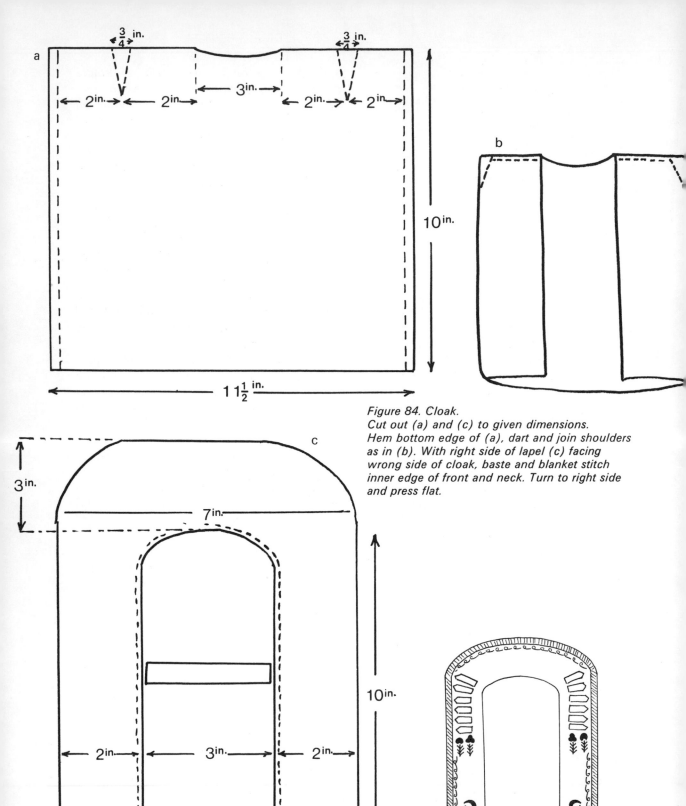

Figure 84. Cloak.
Cut out (a) and (c) to given dimensions.
Hem bottom edge of (a), dart and join shoulders
as in (b). With right side of lapel (c) facing
wrong side of cloak, baste and blanket stitch
inner edge of front and neck. Turn to right side
and press flat.

Figure 85. Cloak embroidery and braiding.

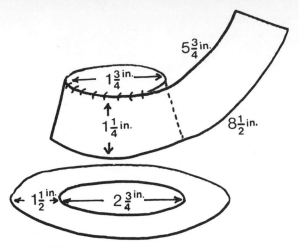

$5\frac{3}{4}$ in.

$1\frac{3}{4}$ in.

$1\frac{1}{4}$ in.

$8\frac{1}{2}$ in.

$1\frac{1}{2}$ in. $2\frac{3}{4}$ in.

Figure 86. Hat.
Cut in felt to dimensions shown. Oversew or
cross-stitch together. Add flower sprig.

Figure 87. Tamas's shirt front embroidery.

Figure 88. Tamas's trouser design.
Embroider before final fitting

Figure 89. Jacket.
Use pattern Figures 73 a–c,
lengthened by $\frac{1}{2}$ in and flared out
at bottom of (a) and (b).

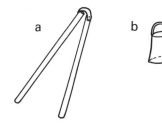

a   b

Figure 91. (a) Flail.
Two candy sticks, joined by a strip of adhesive
plastic. (b) Milk can. A shampoo bottle cap
with wire handle, or made in cardboard, in
the same way as the tambourine (Fig. 42).

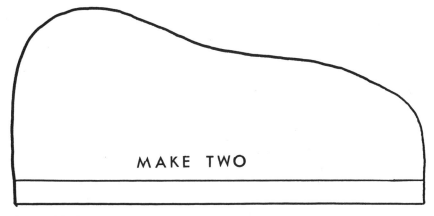

MAKE TWO

Figure 90. Cap.
Adjust size for moulded head doll. Trim with
braid.

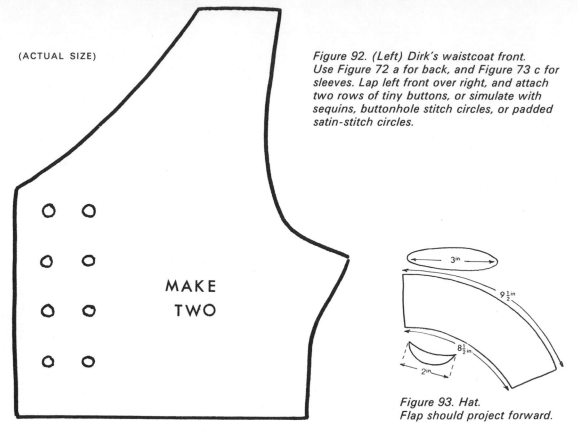

(ACTUAL SIZE)

MAKE
TWO

Figure 92. (Left) Dirk's waistcoat front.
Use Figure 72 a for back, and Figure 73 c for
sleeves. Lap left front over right, and attach
two rows of tiny buttons, or simulate with
sequins, buttonhole stitch circles, or padded
satin-stitch circles.

Figure 93. Hat.
Flap should project forward.

with a band of narrow white embroidery round the neck, to hold the hem flat. The shirt can be white, or any pastel shade. He wears white ribbed, or striped, wool socks. Fawn or gray school socks with a line of wool embroidery down them will do well. On his feet are clogs, either carved or moulded, like *Hendrikje's*.

His trousers are brown, gray or light-coloured wool, or felt, cut in two cylinders and stitched together at the front and leg seams, to make a plump outline. Gather at the ankle and waist, and bind the waist with a strip of the same material, with a silver button, to simulate a waistband.

His jacket is long-sleeved, without lapels, cut to the pattern in Figures 92, 72 a, and 73 c, in a really bright, lightish colour — yellow, green, blue or cerise — in felt, or cloth, allowing small turnings if you use cloth. Make up the waistcoat and lap the left front over the right. Baste into place, and attach a double row of buttons down the front. These can be small silver or gold buttons, or in a contrasting colour. Knot a 7 in strip of

contrasting light material round the neck, with the ends hanging down free, matching the buttons, if appropriate.

Dirk's hat is in dark felt — green, navy, maroon, brown or black. Cut a circle 3 in in diameter, and a strip 3 in wide, flaring from $8\frac{1}{2}$ in long at the bottom to $9\frac{1}{2}$ in at the top. Join this strip into a cylinder, and oversew the top circle to it, gathering the felt slightly to fit. Turn the hat inside out, and the top should bulge upwards a little. Cut a curved flap, as shown in Figure 93, and oversew to the lower edge of the front. Dirk has blond hair, short and close to the head. Use embroidery cotton, with no free ends, as for *Hans* and *Tamas*.

Much of Holland is waterway, so Dirk can carry an oar. Even the cows go by boat to their pastures in some places, so he could also carry a milk bucket, made in cardboard, or a big round Edam cheese with red skin.

Dick the Shepherd (Plate 4)
The English farm labourer wears a white shirt,

like *Hans's* (Figure 69), with the sleeves cut $\frac{1}{2}$ in shorter, and given wrist bands to bind the gathered ends. He wears corduroy breeches, gaiters and ankle boots, and the traditional smock. Decide at the outset whether you are going to smock back and front, or just the front, and if two lots of smocking are too much, cut the back of the smock 2 in narrower, so that it is merely full enough to gather. Make the smock in soft cotton, traditionally off-white or cream for the southern counties, lightish green for East Anglia, light brown for the south Midlands and mid-blue for further north. The material should look washed-out by rain and sun over many years. Embroider in white, cream or light brown cotton.

Cut an oblong of material, $6\frac{1}{2}$ in $\times$ 7 in; hem $\frac{1}{2}$ in at the bottom, and allow $\frac{1}{4}$ in for the arm seam. Start gathering $\frac{1}{2}$ in inside this, working from a $\frac{1}{4}$ in of the top to make a band $1\frac{1}{2}$ in deep. Shirr or hand-gather this, but make sure that the tucks are very tiny, and very even. When the piece is gathered tightly enough to fit across the chest com-

fortably, begin smocking, in regular lines across the gathers, either following a traditional smocking pattern from an embroidery book, or copying the simple design given here. This employs our old friend, feather-stitch, with chain-stitch and zigzag bands. (Figure 94). Work the back in the same way, or gather it to fit. Work a small piece of smocking at the wrist of the sleeve, which is a simple oblong, 6 in $\times$ 3 in, and turn the raw edge under.

Make up a collar (Figure 95) in two sections, and attach its front centre to the front centre of the neck. Cut a tab, $\frac{3}{4}$ in wide, and about $1\frac{1}{2}$ in long, according to the tension of your smocking, measuring the distance from the front shoulder edge to the point where the collar joins the neck. Stitch this tab to the front shoulder and attach the collar to it, leaving sufficient free to cover the back of the neck. Set in the sleeves at the front, leaving enough of the back open to enable the smock to be fitted. Put it on the doll, and complete stitching of shoulder, sleeve and neck.

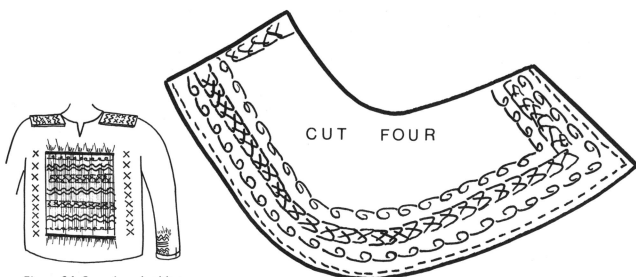

CUT FOUR

Figure 94. Smock embroidery.
Any orthodox smocking pattern can be used, or this simple design, in chain stitch, zigzag and feather stitch, with a line of cross stitch down each side. Gather the material very closely and evenly at the front, and pin to a piece of card, for easier working in straight lines.

Figure 95. Collar.
Make up in two sections, as for Figure 70, and embroider before attaching to smock. The triple embroidered end is placed at centre front slit. Fix as in Figure 70.

Dick wears cream-coloured underpants, like *Ladislas*. The breeches are cut in lightish brown, gray or mossy green corduroy, using the pattern for *Ladislas* (Figure 82) with a $\frac{1}{4}$ in of fullness added all round. Stitch the leg and front seams, fit, and join the back seam. Pull the bottom of the leg tightly to the leg at the knee, and confine the fullness in a small pleat at the side, stitched down and trimmed with cross-laced cord on top, to a depth of $\frac{1}{2}$ in.

He can have socks of dirty white or beige wool (or stockinet), and these will scarcely show. Cut his gaiters of leather — shiny, and as stiff as you can handle. They should fit the leg, edge to edge, almost precisely, so the exact width will depend on your stuffing. The length will be about $2\frac{1}{2}$ in. Spike or drill two lines of holes, a $\frac{1}{4}$ in in from the edge of the gaiter, and cross-lace them with black or brown cord, ending with a small bow. Draw eyelet holes with a black felt-tip pen, and stick tiny pieces of black adhesive plastic on the ends of the bow, to simulate metal tags.

Cut the ankle boots in thin leather, preferably gray or black, but not matching the gaiters, which should be lightish brown. Stitch the sections together visibly, and draw a 'toecap' line where indicated, in the pattern in Figures 74 a–c. Stitch and stuff the toe, and attach the ankle piece to the sole also, but do not join the projecting tongue to the ankle. Attach the boot by stitching through from side to side of the foot on the heel piece line as indicated, but leave the projecting tongue unfastened. Make cross-lacing from just above the 'toecap' to the top of the ankle, tucking the tongue inside the front of the boot. Finish by tying the laces in a bow at the back of the heel.

Dick's hat is a billycock, made of brown or gray felt. Cut a circle 2 in in diameter, and a strip, just under $2\frac{1}{2}$ in wide, and flaring from $7\frac{1}{2}$ in at the top to $8\frac{1}{2}$ in at the bottom. Oversew the circle to the top of the strip, easing in the slight fullness as you go. Stitch the back seam, turn and add a brim, 1 in wide and cut on the bias (diagonally across the cloth). Baste this down, lapping it slightly under the edge of the crown, and gathering a little as you go. The precise length you use will depend on the amount you gather. The finished brim should stick forwards and downwards, at an angle of about 45°, and be irregularly wavy, as if it has been out in years of rainstorms (Figure 96).

Dick carries a shepherd's crook (Figure 97) made from a 12 in length of wood, preferably a fairly straight twig, $\frac{1}{2}$ in in diameter, or dowelling, with a wire hook from a dry cleaner's hanger, curved as shown, fixed in the top, and bound on with twine. An alternative is some kind of cable wire, sold for car electricals, which is flexible enough to shape, but stiff enough to stay put, and comes covered in brown plastic sheathing. He also carries a lamb under his arm, made of wire and cotton wool, or pipe cleaners (Figure 98).

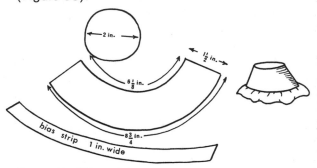

Figure 96. Billycock hat.
Gather and pucker bias strip before stitching on.

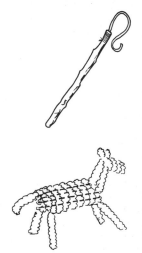

Figure 97. Crook.

Figure 98. Lamb.
Use one pipe cleaner to make skeleton of body and face. Wind second cleaner from rear right leg, round body in spiral to front left leg, and another from rear left leg, round body to front right leg. Use short length from one ear, round face and back to other ear.

72

Elizabeth I and Charles II

Mme de Pompadour and Charles Edward

CHAPTER 8

Some Historical Personages

Once you have mastered the basic techniques of making and dressing costume dolls, you can go ahead to the more elaborate looking historical dolls. These are all constructed using the *Cloth Charles* and *Cloth Charlotte* bodies, adapted where necessary to suit the characters' dimensions. They all have portrait heads, modelled from illustrations of the person, in any of the ways listed in Chapter Three. The possible field of choice is endless and fascinating, and I have selected a handful of historical personages with a distinctive style of dress, from the sixteenth to the nineteenth centuries. I hope you will enjoy making them.

Henry VIII (Plate 6)
Unattractive as he undoubtedly was in person and habits in real life, *King Henry VIII* is a fascinating model to make, because of the sheer magnificence of his clothes. Even on a small scale, those layers and layers of rich fabrics, encrusted with embroidery and jewels, weigh quite a lot, so to display them properly, a wired doll is necessary. Use a *Cloth Charles* pattern, thickened $\frac{1}{4}$ in all round, and a little more in the waist. This still won't look fat enough, but the layers of material mount up disproportionately, and the final effect will be square and heavy. Remember to make the legs fatter, but keep them shapely, because Henry prided himself on his curvy calves, and these show in the Tudor costume style.

Paint, or preferably mould, the head from one of the many Holbein portraits of Henry in about 1537–43. These are to be found in most history books and encyclopaedias and Francis Hackett's book *Henry VIII* gives a portrait and a chalk drawing of his face. His hair is red-gold, and fast-receding from the centre of his scalp, and his beard is darker — a warm, brown crêpe hair is used for this. His hands are to be shown as fat, clenched fists, so thicken the end of the arm pattern, and do not mark full-length fingers on it.

The actual clothes of this reign were in rich velvets or brocades, extensively embroidered, and then slashed all over with little holes, through which the silk undergarments puffed. It is difficult to cut and hem round small enough slashes neatly, so it is best to simulate these by cutting the upper garment in strips and joining these with braid and embroidery across ready-made puffs of under-garment. The strips can be made of velvet, embroidered all over with Tudor knots, or of figured brocade, with a ground colour matching the plain velvet used for the skirt of the doublet. It is sometimes possible to buy brocade trimming, as used in upholstery work to edge sofas and chairs, which looks just right. Whichever material you use, cut it in strips shaped to the pattern in Figures 99 b and d, leaving a $\frac{1}{8}$ in gap between each strip. Pin the strips at this distance apart on a paper tracing of the pattern, and cut out (see Figure 100).

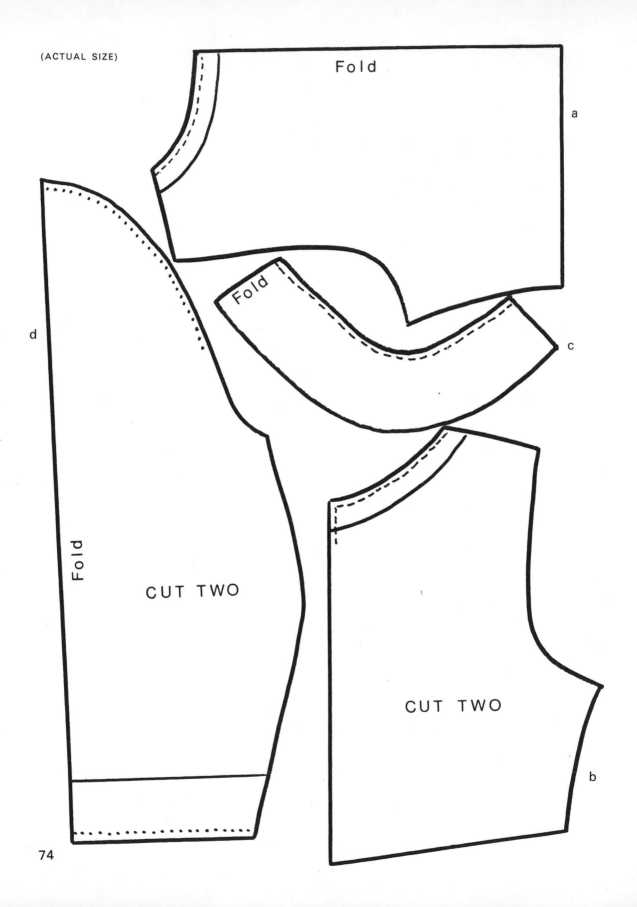

(ACTUAL SIZE)

Fold

a

Fold

c

d

Fold

CUT TWO

CUT TWO

b

74

*Figure 99. (Opposite page) Henry VIII's doublet.
(a) Back. (b) Front. (c) Neck facing.
(d) Sleeve. Cut (a), (c) and skirt
section (16 in × 2½ in) in plain
velvet or joined strips of brocade, the
rest as Figure 100.*

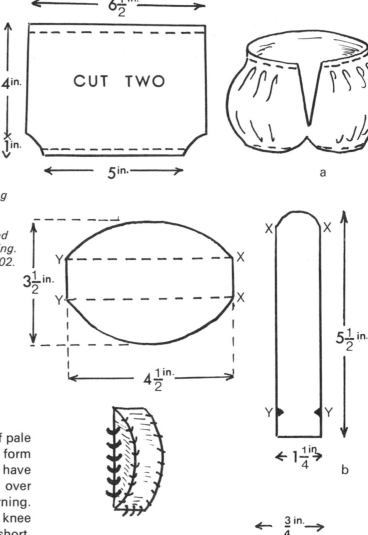

$6\frac{1}{2}$ in.

CUT TWO

4 in.

1 in.

5 in.

a

$\frac{1}{8}$ in. gaps

*Figure 100. Cut Figure
99 (b) and (d) by laying
pattern over hemmed
velvet or brocade strips
placed $\frac{1}{8}$ in apart, pinned
in place on tissue backing.
Make up as in Figure 102.*

$3\frac{1}{2}$ in.

Y   X
Y   X

$4\frac{1}{2}$ in.

X   X

$5\frac{1}{2}$ in.

Y   Y

$1\frac{1}{4}$ in

b

Henry wears stockings to the thigh, of pale
blue (or white) stockinet, Cut these to form
cylinders, and shape them to the leg you have
stuffed, so that they will be skin-tight over
the calf, with the minimum edge turning.
Tie a narrow red ribbon just below the knee
as a garter. Over these go a pair of short,
baggy trunks (Figure 101 a) cut in a firm
rayon, to look like silk, in purple or deep red.
Stitch the side and leg seams, and gather at
the leg and the waist, edging with a narrow
bias strip of the same material. The front is
left open till last, to enable the trunks to be
pulled on, and then joined with a tab on the
outside. This was the codpiece, and, if
you are prepared to cope with the com-
ments, it was actually padded, projected out
of the coat at the front, and was outlined with
ribbons, which secured the top round the
waist. You will see this codpiece in
illustrations of the Holbein portraits, and
Figure 101 b is the pattern for it. If you feel
shy, use Figure 101 c instead.

*Figure 101. (a) Trunks. Cut
out in rayon to dimensions
given, and make up with opening at front. (b) Codpiece.
Cut both sections in rayon
matching trunks. Fold back
section upwards on dotted lines,
stitch front strip to curved
edges, from XX almost to YY,
then stuff evenly. Close at YY
and stitch over trunks opening.
Use contrasting colour for
visible stitches all round, and
embroider in two colours down
front strip. Codpiece should
project in opening of doublet
skirt. (c) Fly-front. Turn under
edges and stitch down front
opening with contrasting colour.*

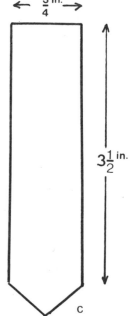

$\frac{3}{4}$ in.

$3\frac{1}{2}$ in.

c

Henry's shirt is white, in fine, thin fabric, and cut according to Figures 69 a–c. The wrist and neck should be pinked or gathered to a hemmed frill. These are the only parts of the shirt which will show, and they may be embroidered with a thin line in black, a $\frac{1}{4}$ in from the edge.

The next garment would be a loose silk waistcoat, matching the trunks, which would show in puffs through the slashes in the upper coat. It is simpler to cut this as a lining to the coat, laying it across the strips when joined, and poking little 'blisters' of the silk through to the right side, then basting the lining invisibly into place (Figure 102).

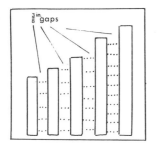

Figure 102. Lay cut strips for pattern Figures 99 b and 99 d on lining material, $\frac{3}{8}$ in apart and cut to shape. Gather lining between strips, and pull 'blisters' of cloth through between velvet. Stitch across lower edge of fronts, and neaten neck edge with appliquéd facing (99c) when garment is made up. Bind sleeve end with braid or embroidered bars.

Cut the back of the doublet (Figure 99 a) in plain blue velvet, embroidered in vertical bands to match the front, or join the brocade strips vertically to fit the pattern without gaps. Cut the front and sleeves in strips, and either tiny hem and embroider the velvet, or make any necessary addition to the brocade strips. Pin the strips on to a sheet of paper, $\frac{1}{8}$ in apart, and join with embroidered or braided bars, to a depth of a $\frac{1}{4}$ in, leaving $\frac{3}{8}$ in gaps for the puffs — or $\frac{1}{2}$ in if the lining is too thick to show well. Try the effect first. The correct embroidery to use is in Beaufort portcullis style (Figure 103), in a square, with loops at each corner, interlaced by a cross, in cord, thin braid or thick embroidery silk. The cross-

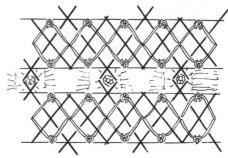

*Figure 103. Beaufort stitch.
Instructions in Chapter Five. Work on fronts and sleeves, taking long fork of herringbone to halfway across the gathered lining. The next set of projecting forks should meet this exactly, forming a lozenge. Fill this with a jewel. Embroider similar design on upper side of skirt pleats only, but do not join the forks.*

pieces can be carried over the gaps to join the strips, as shown.

The front of the doublet, you will find, does not quite meet comfortably around *King Henry's* royal stomach, and it is joined by a strip which simulates two narrow strips linked by braid or embroidery and jewelled clasps. Make this as shown in Figure 104, and baste it to the centre of *Henry's* front when he is dressed. The jewels for clasps can be bought in quantity from some art shops, novelty shops or, more cheaply, from wholesale jewellers as costume jewellery, or they can be detached from the cheap brooches sold by market traders. Sew or glue them in position, surrounded by braid

Figure 104. Front strip. Braid or embroider down both edges. Place line of jewelled clasps down centre.

mountings. If you have enough, then ornament the sleeves and front of the doublet also, between the embroidered frets. Tiny pearls or beads could be substituted for the latter decorations.

Before making up the doublet, baste the puffed lining into position in front and sleeves, holding the puffs by tiny gathers concealed by bars of braid (Figure 102). Cut the bottom skirt of the doublet in plain velvet or joined strips, 16 in long by $2\frac{1}{4}$ in deep. Flat hem the raw edges and make deep box pleats all round. Join it to waist of the doublet, leaving the centre front open. The cod-piece will project here if you have made it that way. Braid or embroider the pleats vertically all round.

The cloak is also made of rich-coloured velvet — dark red, dark green or rich dark blue look well against the pale blue of the doublet. The back and front are oblongs, 5 in × 7 in and 2 in × 7 in, respectively; they are joined for the bottom 5 in at the side and across shoulders (Figures 105 a–d). Cut two sleeve strips, 5 in × 6 in, and turn up a hem 1 in deep on the short side. Gather to fit the sleeve hole, and stitch into place. Do not join the seam at the sides of the cuff, but turn in the raw edge. Embroider a chevron, or appliqué a brocade strip across the puffed sleeve, terminating just above the cuff, and trim the inside of the cuff with embroidery and/or brocade (Figure 106).

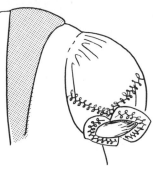

Figure 106. Sleeve embroidery.
Turn back hem at cuff.

Edge the whole front and neck of the cloak with fur, preferably white 'ermine'. This can be created out of white rabbit or fur fabric by marking in black spots with an ink marker. The back collar should be deeper than the front edge, and if you have enough fur, edge the cuffs as well, very thinly. If you have no white fur, use black or brown, but avoid black fur on a black cloak, as this looks too Spanish or sombre. A velvet facing in another colour is possible, though not as authentic.

Henry's hat is made of the same velvet as his cloak, cut from a circle $4\frac{1}{2}$ in in diameter, gathered, to fit the top of the head, and edged with a round brim, cut as shown in Figure 107 a, and trimmed with jewels under the brim, which is turned up, and stitched into position to show them off (Figure 107 b). It should have a white or pale blue 'ostrich feather' curling round above the brim and hanging over one ear. These feathers can be bought from millinery departments of big department stores.

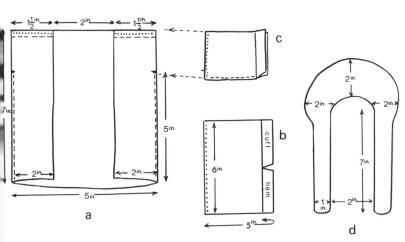

Figure 105. Cloak.
(a) Cut back and fronts to these dimensions, and stitch together, gathering shoulders down to $1\frac{1}{2}$ in (b) Cut sleeves, and make 1 in hem, with slot, on one side. (c) Join underarm seam, and gather sleeve to fit armhole opening. Preferably line whole cloak with silk. Bind front and neck edge with a strip of matching velvet, cut on bias, about 1 in wide. (d) Cut lapel in fur, and line with matching silk or rayon, taking care not to catch hair in stitches. Lay wrong (lining) side of lapel on right side of cloak, and stitch through from lining to bias bound edge, brushing fur over join.

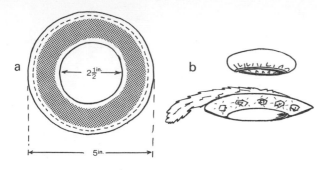

Figure 109. Henry's sword.

Figure 107. Tudor hat.
(a) Cut brim, twice, in velvet, then cardboard stiffener to size of shaded portion. Stitch brim on dotted line, turn and insert stiffener. Hem inner edges together firmly. Gather crown, hem edge and join to brim. (b) Decorate brim, which should slope upwards as shown.

His shoes can be in black felt (or velvet, although this makes the toe slashing harder). Cut to the pattern in Figure 108 a–c. Line the toe, after slashing, with puffed rayon, and fill in the instep with a scrap of pale blue stockinet to match the leg. Ornament with a rosette of red ribbon.

His sword has the hilt shaped in body wire and wound with gold wire, or silver fuse wire and braid, or moulded from papier mâché, and jewel-studded (Figure 109). The scabbard is shiny black plastic, or black felt. The sword can be separately made, or the hilt stuck to the scabbard. Hang the sword from a loose belt of braid or ribbon, over his left hip. His clenched fist rests on this sword belt, and the other is on his right hip, holding a pair of gloves, cut flat in black felt, and embroidered at the cuff. Both hands have 'rings' of jewels on bands of gold.

Anne Boleyn (Plate 6)

Henry is not complete without a wife, very much in the background, and not allowed to compete sartorially. *Anne Boleyn,* his second Queen, stole him from Katherine, and lost her head when he tired of her. She must have been more attractive than the portrait of her in the National Gallery, London, so make her head with an oval face, small mouth and lively dark eyes. Her hair was very dark, and her skin very white. The flat corseting of the

(ACTUAL SIZE)

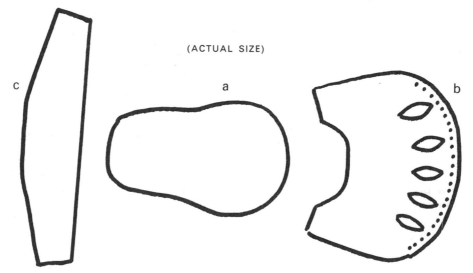

Figure 108. Tudor shoes.
Cut in felt. Fold toe (b) and cut slashes where indicated. Line with rayon to match doublet blisters. Gather edge of (b) slightly to fit sole (a) and stuff well. Attach lower edge of heel (c) to sole, fit on to leg, and fill in instep gap with scrap of stocking material and stuffing.

time eliminated most of the curves from her figure, however, so do not shape the *Cloth Charlotte* body too much in front.

Pantaloons are quite unhistorical at this date, so leave them out, if you wish, and start with white or pastel stockings, to above the knees, and a thin muslin under-petticoat. Over this, *Anne* wore an over-petticoat of rich brocade, in red, or green, figured in gold, silver or black. Upholstery or drapery fabric is best for this; if you can only get a small piece, it would be possible to limit the use to a triangle of brocade, mounted on a cotton petticoat, for this is all that will show.

Her overskirt is in rich velvet, in a dark colour, like wine-red, deep green, warm brown or even black. Both petticoats and the overskirt are cut 8 in deep, by 12 in wide, and gathered to fit the waist at the top. The petticoats are side-seamed, but the overskirt is left open at the front, and trimmed all down the edge with gold ribbon or braid. When fitted, it opens over a triangle of the brocade underskirt, and should be tacked into place at intervals.

The bodice is a flat strip, 1½ in deep by about 6 in — the length which fits tightly around the chest and laps enough to stitch down the back. Cut two short sleeves in the velvet, and pin the bodice and sleeves in place, marking where they will join when pulled close as in Figure 110.

Take them off again, and trim the front and back of the neck and the sleeve tops, which will be exposed, with gold ribbon or braid over the hem, and white ribbon, not gathered, outside the hem edge, as shown. Decorate the outer edge of the ribbon with a line of black embroidery, and stitch seed pearls on the gold braid, in pairs, at as close intervals as you have pearls available, or with paste jewels. Do not stitch the bodice on yet.

Cut an undersleeve of white muslin, 4½ in long by 5 in wide; turn a deep hem, and embroider a border in black. Gather 1 in back from the wrist, and at the top edge, which should fit the short sleeve of the bodice. Cut an upper sleeve in brocade, either matching the over-petticoat, or toning

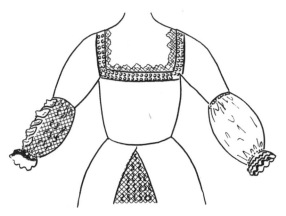

Figure 110. Sleeves cut similarly to Figure 55, but shortened to elbow length, and flattened at top. Mark meeting points of bodice and sleeves, trim separately, ending with diagonals, which join when the garment is fitted. The top of the brocade lower sleeve coincides exactly with the top of the muslin sleeve, and the bottom with the wrist gathers on the muslin sleeve. Join the brocade loosely with bars of stitching, and puff the muslin through the gaps.

with it, 3 in long by 3 in wide. Hem, but do not join the side seam. Gather the top to fit the short sleeve, and bottom to match. Stitch or braid the upper sleeve together over the undersleeve at ½ in intervals, letting the undersleeve puff through. Jewel the joins, and set both sleeves into the short sleeves, with the puffs at the outer side of the arms. Stitch the sleeves and bodice onto the doll, pulling tightly over chest and shoulders.

Make deep cuffs, as in Figure 111, of the

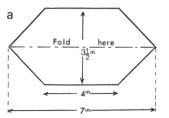

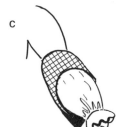

Figure 111. Anne's cuff.
(a) Cut in velvet, fold, and turn in tiny hems. Cover whole cuff, on outside face, with gold net, or trim with fur. Attach narrow end of cuff to velvet upper sleeve at elbow, with point hanging down in line with underarm seam.

dress velvet covered with gold net, or gold lace, or turned with fur — black or brown, not ermine like *Henry's*. Attach these cuffs to the short sleeves, over the undersleeves. Add finger rings — and, if you wish to mystify, draw six fingers on *Anne's* hands, for she is reputed to have suffered from polydactylism.

Her hat is a black hood, cut as in Figure 112 a in black velvet, or satin, with a stiffener of card between the two layers. The front of the hood is trimmed with lace, or pleated nylon frill, and the brim is edged with two rows of small pearls. The loose veil at the back is black georgette or nylon. Place as shown in Figure 112 b.

She also has a pearl necklace, in two loops, with her initial 'B' in gold wire, pendant in the centre, and three pearl drops hanging from it. *Henry* thriftily had these pearls remounted for his next Queen, on a brooch with 'H-J' for *Henry* and Jane. Her shoes, barely visible, are black felt slippers, with slashed toes, like *Henry's*.

Elizabeth I (Plate 7)
Elizabeth, the daughter of *Henry* and *Anne*, was as fond of rich clothing as her father, though she was only half his width. Use a *Cloth Charlotte*, slimmed down, since the flat front corsets were still in vogue. Her face was oval, like her mother's, though more

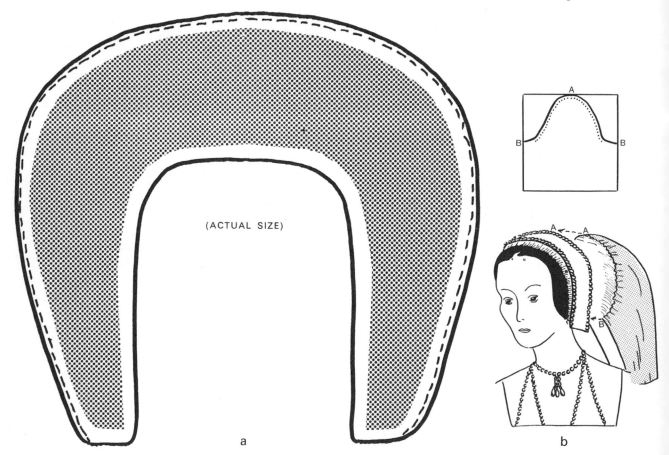

(ACTUAL SIZE)

a

b

Figure 112. French Hood.
(a) Cut twice in velvet or satin, stitch and turn. Line with cardboard stiffener, cut as shaded portion and complete stitching tightly. (b) Trim with two rows of pearls, and a muslin frill at the lower edge.
Cut a loose veil, according to size of head, gather curved section, and attach to back of hood. A should be just below upper edge, and BB almost at corners of lower edge.

bony, and her hair when young was like her father's, red-gold. She lost almost all of it when middle-aged, and is always shown wearing one of her hundreds of wigs, short, bushy, full of curls, and flaming red or yellow. There are many portraits available for making a head and mask.

Dress *Elizabeth* in white or pastel stockinet knee stockings, embroidered at the ankles with 'clocks' (circular designs) and held up by ribbon garters (or a stitch). Instead of pantaloons, give her a white muslin petticoat, like *Anne's*. Her next underwear is a great farthingale, which was a structure of whalebone, buckram and tapes, to hold out her dress. Make this in wire, like a squashed wheel. The hub of the wheel is the circumference of the hips, $\frac{1}{2}$ in below the waist, in a somewhat oval shape. The spokes radiate from this, 2 in long, at most, to the rim of the wheel, also oval in shape. Wire up three-quarters of the wheel, as shown in Figures 113 a–b, then fit it to the body, and join the front section. Add a reinforcing twist of wire where necessary.

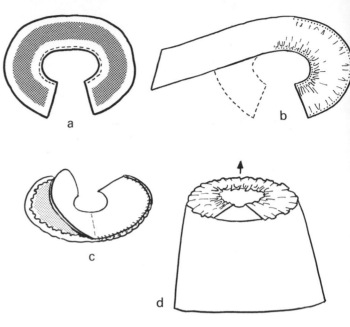

Figure 114. Farthingale petticoat.
Cut one pattern (a) in cotton, and a cardboard stiffener as shaded portion. (b) Gather bias strip to fit (a), turn its edge over the cardboard, and hem the flat cover (a) tightly to it. Leave front triangle unfilled. Fit to doll, tilting back of farthingale higher than front. (d) Cut skirt of petticoat to fit lengths thus formed at back and front. Stitch on skirt, and fill in triangle with loosely gathered cotton, to take point of stomacher.

The farthingale had buckram and tapes to help hold up the dress, and this is best simulated by a stiffened petticoat. Cut a three-quarter farthingale in stiff cardboard, and a cotton cover, $\frac{1}{4}$ in larger all round. Gather a $2\frac{1}{2}$ in bias strip to fit the shape, trimming shorter at the back to fit the oval. Run a second line of retaining stitches round the outer circumference of the gathers, and oversew the edge of the flat cover to the edge of the gathered cover, stitching them tightly around the cardboard (Figures 114 a–d). Tilt the whole farthingale so that it is slightly higher at the back than the front. Add a skirt to the farthingale cover, lightly gathered, 7 in long at the back, and shorter at the front, by the amount of the tilt. Fill in the triangle left in the front cover with a loosely gathered piece of cotton.

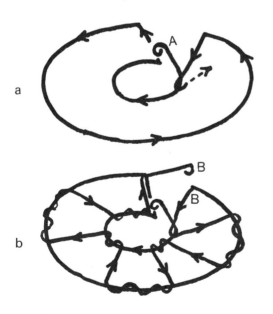

Figure 113. Farthingale.
Wire from centre outwards, starting at A and following arrows. Complete by joining A to inner waistline and BB in outer ring, when fitted to doll.

81

The overskirt is cut in much the same way. There is no under-cover, but the upper farthingale is cut from a bias strip, 2½ in wide at the sides, lessening slightly at the back, and also at the front, since it covers the unstiffened section there. It is gathered into deep box pleats, except at the front, where the pleat is much shallower over the soft section. The opening in the cover for fitting can conveniently be made at the back, and covered by a box pleat. Hem the outer edge of the farthingale before pleating, with a ¼ in hem, which will project over the lower skirt when joined. The lower skirt is cut basically 8 in long, trimmed shorter in the front, and given a ½ in hem at the bottom.

The material for this skirt should be heavily embroidered, in diagonal patterns, with jewels at most of the intersections. Unless you happen to discover a suitable piece of brocade with heavy gold-thread 'embroidery' in its pattern, in which case you can just stitch diagonals across it, and add jewels, I suggest using a quilted nylon as a base — with the wadded backing, it looks like satin padded with calamanca, and gives you straight lines to work on. Embroider in chain-stitch, or attach braid or cord down each diagonal, and at every intersection, 1 in apart, stitch or braid a diamond shape, and insert a tiny jewel in it. For best results, also hang a pearl beneath the jewel. If you are short of jewels, gold wire, gold braid or a sequin will substitute, or a tiny shiny glass bead. Choose a light or delicate colour for your background, and embroider in a toning colour — e.g. gold on white, pale blue on pale green. You cannot overdo the decoration here. The actual farthingale need only be decorated with jewels on the bits that show — the upper sides of the pleats, with embroidery linking them. The outer edge should be trimmed with braid, a ¼ in in, either matching that on the skirt, or toning.

The bodice is made in two sections — the overdress, which matches the skirt, and the stomacher. Cut the overdress as shown in Figure 115 a and decorate. Cut the triangular stomacher to Figure 115 b in a contrasting

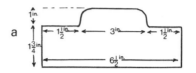

Figure 115. (a) Bodice.
Adjust to fit doll skin-tight. The raised section forms the back. (b) Stomacher. Top should be level with top of bodice, point juts down into skirt.

fabric, either a dark rich satin, or velvet, or fine sateen, lined with white or light cotton, and, if it is not stiff enough, with an inner cotton lining. The whole thing should also be decorated, in horizontal bands across the chest, with rows of braid in curling patterns, strips of gold lace or ribbon, or broad embroidery in rich colours, and studded with jewels like a row of clasps down the centre front. When the stomacher is iron stiff (they were lined with iron corset plates in real life) set it with its point sticking downwards into the unstiffened portion of the farthingale top, and stitch it, and the overdress, into position (Figure 116). Make the join at the front, covering the stitching with a row of braid as used round the farthingale, taking it right to the point of the stomacher.

Cut sleeves (Figure 99 d) from the stomacher material, and edge the wrists with broad lace. Make banana-shaped epaulettes of the overdress fabric to fit over the shoulders, stuff them with cotton and band with dark braid, the colour of the stomacher (Figure 117). Attach these over the bodice shoulders, and join to them a length of the overdress material, as a hanging sleeve, 11 in long by 3 in wide, lined with white or same colour in silky material. Attach the inner sleeve, so it is framed by this outer hanging sleeve (Figure 118). Trim the edge of the hanging sleeve with braid.

Around her neck is a ¾ in deep small ruff, of frilled organdie, or a larger, open-fronted ruff, of broad lace, three layers of either (Figures 119 a and b). Behind the head is a heart-shaped organdie collar, wire stiffened,

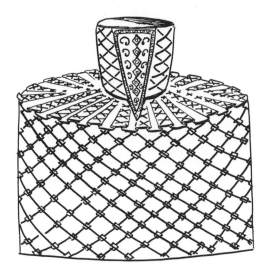

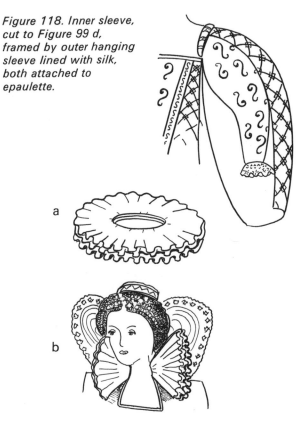

Figure 118. Inner sleeve, cut to Figure 99 d, framed by outer hanging sleeve lined with silk, both attached to epaulette.

a

b

Figure 116. The outer dress.
Braid along diagonals or embroider at 1 in intervals. Add jewels and pendant pearls at intersections. Only the outer folds of the farthingale top need be decorated. The stomacher, in darker material, has braided edge and curls of embroidery over all, plus a line of jewelled clasps down the centre.

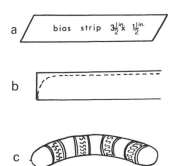

a   bias strip 3½in x 1½in.

b

c

Figure 117. Epaulettes.
(a) Cut bias strip of dress material. (b) Fold, stitch side and one end, turn inside out and stuff lightly to banana shape. (c) Bind with braid and stitch across shoulder of dress.

Figure 119. (a) Closed ruff.
Three layers of stiffened lace or organdie, gathered directly to the neck, or on a tape band, open at the back and secured later, when fitted. (b) Open ruff, of three layers of softer organdie or broad lace. Gather on two tape bands, and anchor lightly to front and back of bodice, tacking outer edge of under layer to epaulette. The heart-shaped collar at the back of the head is cut from figured muslin, stiffened with spray starch or wired, with anchor points on the shoulders and back of the head.

standing up high above the hair, lace edged and jewelled, mounted on the collar, or wired from the shoulders. On her head is a tiny velvet cap, jewelled like a crown (Figure 120). She also has a jewelled necklace, with a pendant of wire and a large stone, with any amount of 'pearl' ropes hanging across her front.

She carries gloves, embroidered and jewelled, cut flat like her father's, in one hand, and in the other a fan, bought as a Christmas novelty, or made of wire and paper. She wears

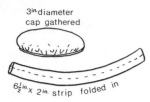

3in.diameter
cap gathered

6½in.x 2in. strip folded in

Figure 120. Jewelled cap. Finished seam of strip is located centrally inside head band. Gathered crown is stitched to the brim at seam level, leaving upper edge of brim projecting.

when he was on the run after the capture of his father. When his natural hair thinned, he wore huge, dark wigs, with a mop of bushy curls down past the shoulder, just like a King Charles spaniel. His features are bold and imperious, his eyes dark, and he has a narrow line of moustache, for all the world like a plumper Clark Gable. Use a *Cloth Charles,* with well padded calves.

The 'Merry Monarch' preferred rich, rather dark but not sombre, colours — wine-red, plum, dark green, rich brown, purple, mauvy blue, black — so use any combination of these, in silky rayon, sateen or georgette for the breeches and waistcoat, sateen or velvet for the upper coat, and velvet for the cloak.

His shirt, in fine white muslin, is cut to the pattern in Figures 69 a–c. The neck is gathered, and has a broad collar, dealt with later. The sleeve should be edged with broderie anglaise, or broad lace, and gathered above this at the wrist, and again just below the elbow. Tie a ribbon bow, in the breeches colour, round the arm at this point. The breeches are cut from the *Ladislas* pattern (Figure 82) in, say, wine red, fitting tightly at the knee. The stockings, also tight, are in the second colour — say, green — and at the top is a broad frill, in organza, lace-edged muslin or paper nylon, dyed to match the

a loose gold or silver girdle around her waist, and from it can hang a ball pomander (papier mâché), tiny scissors, a scent phial, a mirror — or any similar small novelty that you have collected. She wears black sateen or felt shoes with high heels (Figures 121 a–c). Insert a wedge of cork in the heel section.

And there is Her Royal Majesty, dressed for a quiet day at home with her courtiers, before changing into elaborate clothes for the evening reception.

Charles II (Plate 7)
'A long, dark-haired man, above two yards high' was how the Puritans described him

Figure 121. Court slippers. Join (a) sole to (b) toe, stiffen with card insole and stuff. Stitch lower edge of heel (c) to sole, fit to leg and finish stitching the instep. Cut small round heel support in cork, and spike to foot.

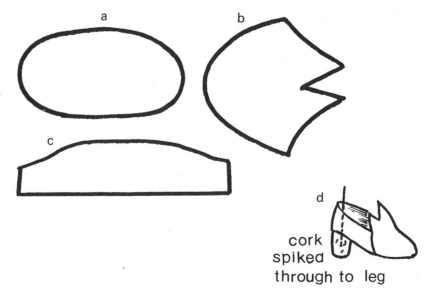

a

b

c

d

cork
spiked
through to leg

stockings. Make it 1 in deep, and about 8 in long, to stand out to about twice leg width on either side. This fashion made a short, fat-legged man look like a carthorse.

The breeches are covered with a huge skirt, 5 in long and 12 in wide, which should be boxed-pleated to fit at the waist. The lower hem just skims the top of the frills, offering fascinating glimpses of the breeches leg. Cut this piece, which gave the garment the name of petticoat-breeches, in green.

Make a short bolero jacket (Figure 77) also in green, which, when made up, leaves a gap between it and the breeches. Fill this gap by stitching ribbon bows, in matching green, or in red, across the gap, as if holding up the breeches. The next garment was a jacket, worn with sleeves, or sleeveless with a cloak. We will have it sleeveless, in wine 'silk' or velvet, cut from the bolero pattern, extended as shown in Figure 122 with a flare to the lower edge. Make a row of buttons all down one side, and button-holes down the other, but do not close the coat. The buttons can be gold, silver or black, and the button-holes are short strips of braid, matching the buttons, with a con-trasting line of stitches for the 'hole'.

The cloak is a circle of blue velvet, 8 in in radius, lined with a circle of the green material. Gather the neck edge until it fits from front collar-bone to front collar-bone, then make a back collar to fit, also in blue velvet. The cloak, and the 'petticoat' skirt can be trimmed all round, ½ in from the edge, with two rows of

black cord, or one of black braid. Try the cloak on the doll, and mark where the left front falls across the arm. Here, just above elbow level, make a badge in gold or silver braid. On a circle of the braid, embroider the motto "Honi soit qui mal y pense", punctuated by small circles. Ideally, embroider in metallic thread, silver on gold, dark gold on light, etc., or use black (Figure 123).

Figure 123. Badge. Make circle and cross of gold or silver braid and embroider in con-trasting metallic thread or black. Decorate with tiny beads, or coloured knots.

Trim the neck with a broad collar, over the cloak, about 2 in deep. Make this of organdie with a deep lace edge or broderie anglaise, or thick lace sold for bridal dresses. Under this, barely visible, was a thick gold chain, fastened with a cameo clasp, and a gold and enamel pendant. Often *Charles* wore a fish pendant, to symbolise his return from across the sea after exile during the time of Cromwell's Commonwealth.

Fix his thick curly wig (Figure 124) on his

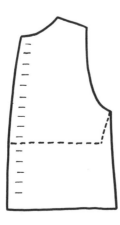

Figure 122. Long waistcoat.
Use pattern Figures 72 a and 77, extended as shown. Make a line of button-holes from strips of braid down whole of left front, and buttons all down right front. Use embroidered circles or spirals of gold or silver wire to simulate tiny buttons.

Figure 124. Make wig in crêpe hair, well frizzed out, or with a lot of curls and ringlets. Make hat as in Figure 75, measuring dimensions of head plus thick wig.

head, and measure the circumference for a hat. Cut a circle, a third of the circumference less ½ in, and a strip 2 in deep, fitting this circle at the top, and flaring to the head size at the bottom. Cut a brim to fit, from a hollow circle 1 in wide, and make up, by oversewing the joins. Cover the brim/crown join with a broad blue ribbon bow.

Charles wears a sword, with a basket hilt (Figure 125), made of metal foil over

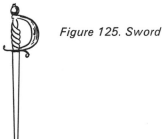

Figure 125. Sword

wire. This is slung on a red ribbon, across his right shoulder, and under his left arm, sticking out behind — to the danger of his own calves, and passing strangers. The sword hanger is under his cloak, which gets hitched up round the hilt. He carries a long black cane with a gold or silver (foil) knob, and a fur muff, attached to one hand. His shoes are black leather Court shoes (Figures 126 a–d) with a silver buckle, set with jewels if you have a suitable tiny brooch.

Figure 126. Court shoes (basic). Join (a) sole to (b) toe, stiffen with card insole and stuff. Attach bottom of heel piece (c), fit to leg, and stitch at instep. Cut half-round cork heel, paint black and spike to sole.

Madame de Pompadour (Plate 8)

La Pompadour was the mistress of Louis XV and of France for many years in the eighteenth century, and she looked and dressed the part. She was a dainty little beauty with a well-developed personality, which she was not averse to displaying, so make her from a *Cloth Charlotte* model, with head and shoulders cast in one, or the bosom and face covered with pale pink satin — nearly white, with rouge patches.

If you wish, give her knee-length pantaloons, trimmed with lace at hem and above it. Otherwise, start with a 7 in deep muslin petticoat, trimmed with a gathered frill of lace or muslin. Over this place a hooped petticoat, made in white cotton, 8 in deep by 15 in wide. Gather this at the waist, and, working on the wrong side, make a circle of wire at the bottom, almost the full width of the skirt, baste this to the hem of the petticoat, and cover the wire with a band of narrow white tape. Make three more hoops, in reducing widths, at 2 in intervals, casing them with tape in the same way. The top is unstiffened, and should be left open at the side for fitting to the doll. Turn the petticoat the right way before securing it to the waist.

Cut an underskirt, 8 in × 16 in, in a rich, light shade — apple green, sky blue, mauve or gold — and gather it to fit over the hoop.

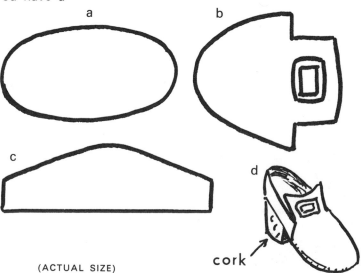

a   b

c

d

cork

(ACTUAL SIZE)

Before stitching it on, make a flounce of the same material, 3 in deep by 14 in wide, cut its bottom edge into gentle curves with pinking shears if possible, or make a tiny hem, and gather the top closely, to fit across the front of the underskirt, 4 in above the hem.

Take a strip of the same material, 1 in wide, turn in the edges with small hems, and gather both top and bottom, very closely. Attach this ruching to the top of the flounce. Make more of this ruching, and outline the edge of the flounce, $\frac{1}{2}$ in above its hem (Figure 127).

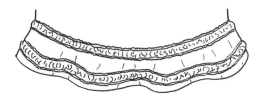

Figure 127. Flounce, with ruched bands.

The overskirt is made of the same material, cut 10 in deep by 20 in wide. Hem the bottom and sides with $\frac{1}{4}$ in hems, and the top minutely. Gather the skirt in matching cotton, vertically, from the lower hem to within 2 in of the top, at 2 in intervals, making the skirt level with the underskirt at the lower edge of the curves. (Figures 128 a and b). Gather from the front edges of the skirt, at the bottom

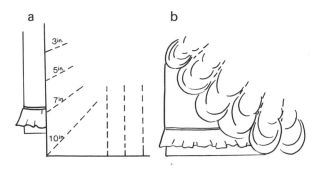

Figure 128. Madame's skirt.
(a) Gather from edge at intervals shown.
(b) Pull up tight and fasten on wrong side.
Low point of rear puffs show coincide with hem of under-skirt.

corner, and at 3, 5 and 7 in above the hem, diagonally upwards for a distance of 4 in, except for the top gather, which should be 2 in.

Make furbelows in a second colour — pink for blue, mauve or green, and white for gold — either in wide ribbon, or in silky material. Ribbon should be pleated fatly and stitched down the middle (Figure 129). The material

Figure 129. Ribbon furbelows.
If strips of material are used, pink edges, or tiny hem both sides.

should be 2 in wide, have the raw edges turned well in, and can either be stitched down the middle, or ruched, which tends to look better. Edge the whole of the overskirt, and the front of the underskirt, with these pink furbelows, curving with the gathered curves, and making a rosette at each indentation. Also furbelow the flounces, between the self-coloured ruches.

Cut a stomacher, lower at the front than *Elizabeth's*, according to how you have stuffed the body. The top edge, when trimmed with a narrow lace frill, should be just decent, but only just. Make the stomacher in white, if your ribbon colour is pink, and pink if it is white, and line it, but do not stiffen it. Trim with a ladder of ribbon bows, very small at the bottom, and very broad at the top, and catch the backs of them into place, if they droop. Use pink ribbon, matching or toning with the furbelows, on green, blue or mauve, or white on gold. Cut a back bodice, like *Elizabeth's* (Figure 115) of the skirt material, attach to the stomacher, and stitch the whole thing into position, trimming the front edge of the back bodice with pink furbelow, if your ribbon exactly matches, or same-coloured ruching, if not.

Cut the sleeves to pattern Figure 130, edging the bottom with 2 in ruching, in the skirt colour, and a pink (or white) large rosette, of gathered ribbon or silk, over the elbow. Trim with a triple frill of broad lace,

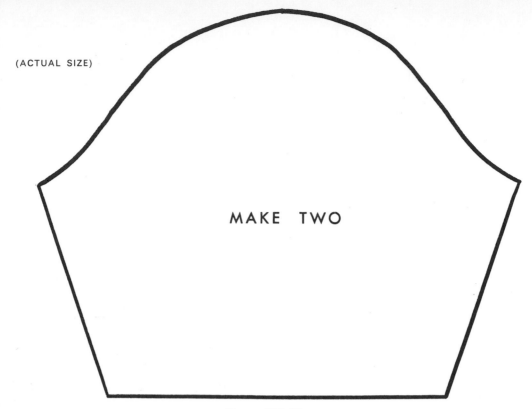

(ACTUAL SIZE)

MAKE TWO

Figure 130. Sleeve.

falling over the lower arm. Set in the sleeve, and trim the top edge with ruching to match the front. Place a large ribbon bow, matching the stomacher, around the throat. This will cover any join between the head and the satin 'bosom', if you make them separately. *La Pompadour* carries a fan, and has silver bracelets.

Make a white wig, from crêpe hair, in the Pompadour style (Figures 25 a and b), padding well out with cotton wool. The wig could be done in fine white embroidery silk also. Top the whole headdress with three ribbon bows, in skirt colour, a pink rosette, and a scrap of fine lace behind them. Twist some pearls, or a jewel pendant hung from fine gold chain or wire, in the front hair, and tip off with an 'ostrich feather' at the back.

Madame wears silk stockings, with fine black embroidery, in white or dress colour, and court shoes.

Bonnie Prince Charlie (Plate 8)
Charles Edward, the 'romantic' Jacobite

Pretender of 1745, is depicted at the height of his youthful fascination — a slim, fair man, with baby blue eyes and well stuffed calves. He wears a white wig, made in hair or embroidery cotton, in the standard style with three side curls, and the rest of the hair drawn back and held in a blue ribbon (Figure 131).

Charlie wears the same loose sleeved shirt as his great-uncle, *Charles II*, gathered in a deep frill at the wrist, and puffing out of his coat sleeve. He may wear short silk drawers — the pantaloons cut at the thigh — and his stockings should be tartan, on a small scale. If this is unobtainable, try drawing the checks in felt-tip, or embroider lines on red ground. The stockings are edged at the knee with short

Figure 131. Wig.
Pad front top section, and add
curls and ringlets in white
crêpe or embroidery silk.

loops of ribbon — just over 1 in long, doubled and stitched flat to the sock, with a small ribbon bow as a garter. The ribbons should be red, green and blue, for Stewart.

His kilt must be tartan, and Royal Stewart at that. It is described as 'red ground, with green and blue wide and narrow crossings, bright blue narrow lines, and over-checks of white and yellow'. This is fortunately readily available wherever tartan is sold, but the woollen kilt weights are too thick. You may find a dress weight for women or children, thinner and even smaller scaled, which would be ideal. Cut a strip, 5 in long, and hem the bottom, with a single turn of the cloth only. Deliberately fray one front edge, to a depth of $\frac{1}{2}$ in, and then secure this fringe with a line of invisible stitching. This will lie on the front left hip. Mark off $1\frac{1}{4}$ in, then start pleating, making the pleats not less than $\frac{1}{4}$ in, or more than $\frac{3}{8}$ in wide, according to the thickness of your material. Stitch the top $1\frac{1}{2}$ in of each pleat down on the outside, and press the rest to a knife edge when you have finished. Pleat around the hips and back, and, when the pleats meet the fringe, complete with a second flat piece, which goes under the fringed edge. Tape the whole kilt at the waistband.

Place a length of white muslin, folded, around his neck, and wind this muslin like a throat bandage, two and a half times. Stitch it tight. Add a three-layer broad lace cravat, gathered to fit the front of the band (Figure 132). This will hang over the jacket.

Figure 132. Cravat.
Three layers of wide lace, staggered on tape backing, and attached to neck band.

The waistcoat is a pale pastel brocade — cream, biscuit, white, pale gold. If it is not figured, decorate it down the front edges in line embroidery, in pale colours plus black. Trim with braid, same-coloured, or a little deeper in tone. Cut from Figures 73a

and 133. Line the front with small pearl (white) buttons, and tiny taped 'holes', of which all but the top two, and those below the waist, are closed. Make 'pocket flaps', $\frac{1}{2}$ in × 1 in, edge them with braid, and stitch on the lower front. Add two small buttons and 'holes'.

The coat is in velvet, preferably sky-blue, or apple green. Cut as in Figures 73 a–c. Line

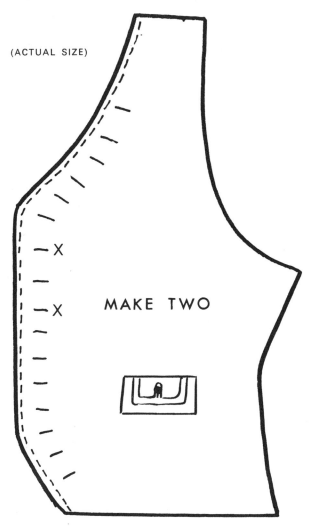

(ACTUAL SIZE)

MAKE TWO

Figure 133. Waistcoat.
Use pattern Figure 73 a for back. Make tape 'button-holes' all down left front and place tiny pearl (white) or embroidered buttons down right front, where indicated, except between XX. Here, lap left side over right, and place buttons on top of taped holes.

it with brocade or pastel 'silk' lining in a plain colour. Edge with silver buttons, and silver braid button-holes, but do not attempt to close any of them, leaving the front widely open. The cuffs are cut from strips, $3\frac{1}{2}$ in wide by 2 in deep, folded in half, gathered slightly to fit the sleeve edge, and stitched in place. The folded edge is then turned back over the sleeve, trimmed with silver braid, and attached in four places with silver buttons. A pocket flap, $\frac{3}{8}$ in $\times$ $1\frac{1}{8}$ in, is stitched to the lower front on both sides, outlined with silver tape, and 'buttoned', in the same way (Figure 134).

Button

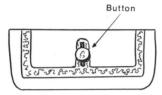

Figure 134. Pocket flap.

From his left shoulder diagonally across his chest, *Charles Edward* wears a blue ribbon, of the Order of the Garter. On the left breast of his coat, he wears the royal sunburst brooch, with "Honi Soit Qui Mal Y Pense" and a red cross of St George on it (Figure 135). This can be cut in cardboard, and painted, or it may be found as a ready-made metal brooch, to which the motto can be added.

Figure 135. Badge. Embroider, as for Figure 123, or cut in card, covered with foil, and paint on lettering.

From his right shoulder, across his left hip, outside his coat, he wears a leather sword hanger, decorated with gold or silver studs, and with a matching large buckle. The sword is basket hilted, like *Charles II's*, with a filigree gold wire 'cage' added round

the hand grip. The sword, in its scabbard, sticks out behind him. On both shoulders, at the front, he wears a large red rosette of ribbon. His shoes are black leather and buckled, like *Charles II's*.

At the front of his kilt he wears a sporran, like a fur purse, in ermine, or black. Cut it like Gipsy *Rosina's* hanging purse, but $\frac{1}{4}$ in smaller, and add a bar clasp and dangling tassels in silver. The sporran is hung round his hips from a thin leather strap, and shows in the opening of his waistcoat. Next to it, or in the top of his stocking, he wears a dirk, a short dagger with a bright silver, pointed blade and a slightly curved horn handle.

Queen Victoria (Plate 9)

Victoria, despite her forbidding reputation, was quite a gay young woman before she lost her husband in 1861. Make her then in 1860, when her only complaint, after a day's pony-trekking in the Scottish Highlands in the rain, was that the meal at an inn was "two starved Highland chickens, no pudding and no *fun*." Considering that she rode, and forded rivers, in the kind of costume below, this was real endurance.

Cut her from the *Cloth Charlotte* pattern, increased in every dimension by years of child-bearing. Make a portrait head of her at around 41, not an old lady's head. The hair is middle brown, parted in the centre, and drawn back to her ears, where it was confined in short plaits, bent round in the ugly 'earphone' style. There are plenty of illustrations of this.

She wears long pantaloons, trimmed with lace at the hem, and above the hem, and a thin muslin under-petticoat. Her stockings are white silk, with patterns woven into them down the front of the leg — a child's sock will make them. Over this went her crinoline petticoat, make like the hooped petticoat for *Madame Pompadour*, but with three hoops in the bottom third of the skirt only, to give a bell-shaped silhouette, rather than a pumpkin shape. Cut the petticoat 8 in deep by 13 in wide in white cotton, tape wires to it at the base, and at just under $1\frac{1}{2}$ in intervals above, on the outside of the garment this time. Then cover the wired area with a strip of bright red cotton. Make a second, quilted over-petticoat in a pastel shade, with an unobtrusive floral pattern — the nylon sold for demure negligées has the right kind.

Make the dress in taffeta or silky rayon, since the trimming will disguise the hems. The colour can be light, but not pastel — a rose or rust red, lilac, mauve, soft ochre — and trimmed with ribbon, braid and fringe in brown or black. The ribbon could match the material, if available. Thick upholstery fringing sometimes comes with a wide braid edge, and this would substitute for both trims where specified.

Cut the overskirt 9 in × 20 in, and box pleat at the waist, with most of the fullness in the back and sides. Make flounces, 2 in deep, and stitch all round the dress, $2\frac{1}{8}$ in above the hem, and the same distance above that again. Trim the flounces with same colour or black or brown narrow ribbon, in velvet or satin finish. The skirt hem may also be edged with ribbon. Cut 2 in slits in the sides of the skirt at the hips, and attach two small pockets (Figure 136).

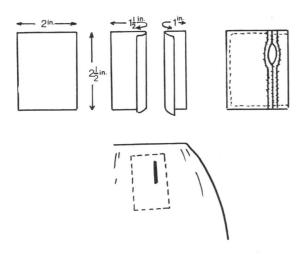

Figure 136. Pocket.
Cut skirt material to these dimensions. Turn back edges of smaller pieces, hem, and join them, leaving 1 in opening near top. Stitch sides together and lay completed pocket inside skirt. Cut slit in skirt to match opening, and turn in raw edges.

The bodice is complicated, beginning with a close fitting upper section. Cut this to Figures 137 a–b, with the back in one piece, and the front open, and dart to fit at the waist. The depth of the dart will vary slightly, according to the precise size of your doll, but make the fit tight. Turn a narrow facing at the front edges. Cut the basque (Figure 137 cd) in two sections, and line with matching, or white, material. Dart the basque sections to fit the waist as well, and join the bodice to basque, stitching or taping the seam quite flat at the waist.

Cut the shoulder wings (Figure 138 a), lining them in same colour or white, and trimming the outer curve with thick black (or brown) braid and fringe. If possible, the fringe should be longer towards the centre of the curve, but this is not practicable unless you can get two lengths of matching fringe, and grade the lengths. After the sleeve is in position, stitch the upper edge of the wing to the shoulder of the under-bodice, so that the lower edge and fringe will hang free over the top of the arm (Figure 138 b). Cover the join with flat ribbon.

Cut the bodice sleeve (Figure 139) and, before seaming, trim the hem with a band of ruched lace or net, matching the dress, or off-white. Above this, add two rows of braid and fringe, one above the other, and both above the net. Make up, and attach sleeves at the shoulder. Add a net or lace under-sleeve, in off-white, made from a cylinder $2\frac{1}{2}$ in deep by 3 in wide, gathered at both ends, and attached under the top sleeve at elbow level. Stitch shoulder wings in place, meeting at the back, and to the edge at the front. Cut the triangular tails (Figure 138c), double them, and turn in raw edges. Trim the diagonal with braid and narrow fringe, the bottom with braid and wide fringe, and the longer, straight side with flat ribbon. With the ribboned edges almost meeting at centre back, stitch the tails at the waist, and with retaining stitches, so that they appear to be continuing the line of the wings, in a cross shape (Figure 138 d).

The basque is braided and fringed (deeply),

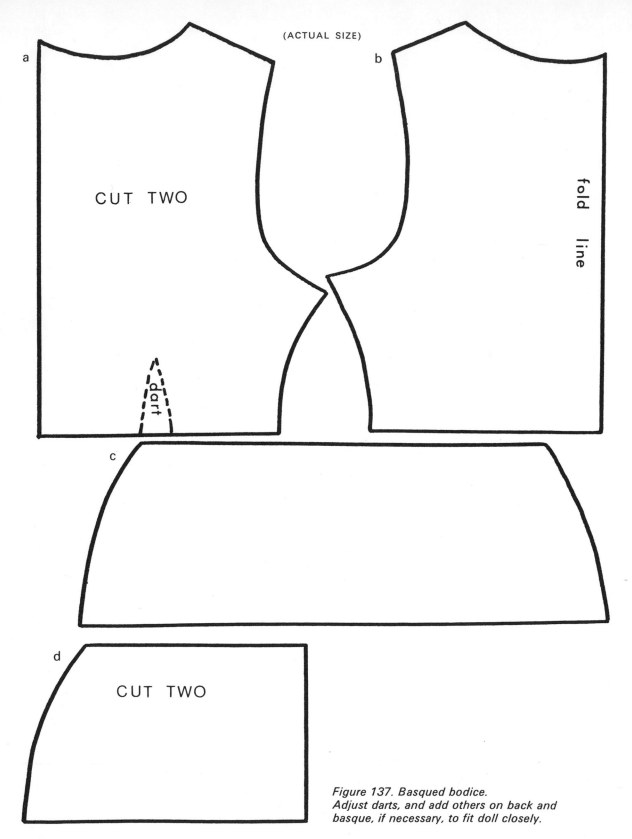

(ACTUAL SIZE)

a

b

CUT TWO

fold line

dart

c

d

CUT TWO

Figure 137. Basqued bodice.
Adjust darts, and add others on back and
basque, if necessary, to fit doll closely.

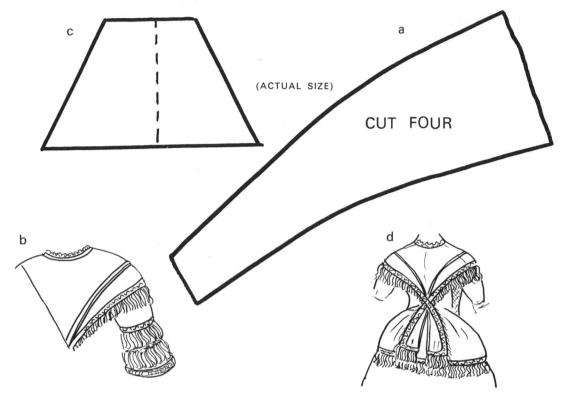

c

(ACTUAL SIZE)

a

CUT FOUR

b

d

Figure 138. Wings and tails.
(a) Cut four in bodice fabric and four in firm lining. Join, turning in all raw edges, and covering with braid and/or fringe. (b) Attach inner edge of wing to bodice as shown, leaving outer edge to hang free over shoulder. (c) Tails. Fold on dotted line, and turn in raw edges. (d) Attach and trim with braid and fringe, continuing line from opposite wing. Back view finished.

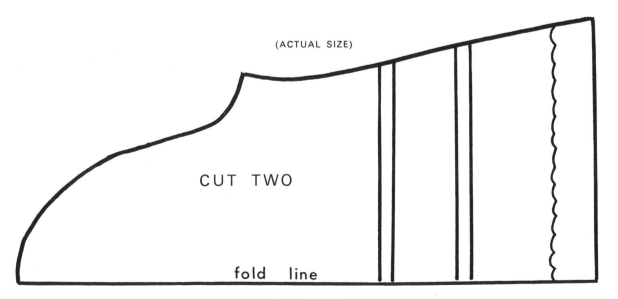

(ACTUAL SIZE)

CUT TWO

fold line

Figure 139. Sleeve.
Attach ruched lace on curved line and two rows of braid and fringe on double lines before making up.

along the bottom and up the centre fronts. Join the front of the bodice from neck to waist, covering this join with a double band of white ribbon, medium and wide, tightly gathered down the middle, and given pearl buttons at intervals (Figure 140). Trim the neck in off-white net or lace, gathered.

Figure 141. Straw bonnet.
(a) Layout of straw plait pieces. Lap each row and bind ends with matching blanket stitching, if necessary. (b) Fill scoop of bonnet with frills of gathered lace and bunches of flowers or cherries on top of this. (c) Trim the brim with rows of ruched lace over straw joins. Place lace frill and ribbon bow on back.

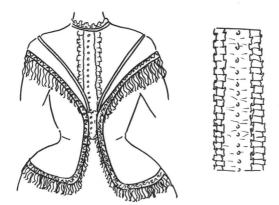

Figure 140. Front view, finished, with detail of ribbon trimming.

The hat is small, and sits on top of the head. If you can obtain flat plaited straw, which is sometimes sold for making table mats, or remove a piece from an old table mat, then make a straw bonnet to your own design, or roughly as below. Plaits vary in width and stiffness, so adapt these instructions freely.

Cut a 6 in strip of plait, and stitch to one edge, lapping minimally, a slightly larger strip, keeping two ends level, and easing a little fullness in at the centre. Repeat, until you have a 1½ in deep, slightly curved strip. Then, working from the middle, make a peak, with short lengths increasing in size until it is possible to edge the bonnet smoothly (Figure 141 a). Line it with white rayon, trim the underside of the brim with gathered net or lace, and stitch a bunch of tiny artificial flowers, or ribbon rosebuds, or coloured lace, between the peak and the hair. Band the upper side of the brim and the crown with coarse lace. Make a frill of this lace, and stitch it to the back of the bonnet (which is filled in with short strips of straw plait). Add a dress-coloured ribbon bow at the centre back,

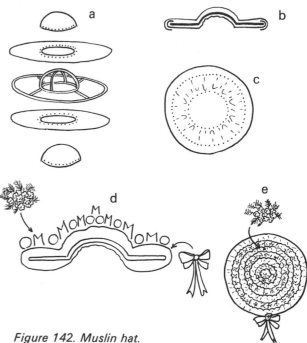

Figure 142. Muslin hat.
(a) Make wire frame on same principle as farthingale (Figure 113), covering tightly with brim and crown covers, attached to outer and inner wire rings. (b) Overlap brim covers round outer wire and hem top tightly over bottom one. (c) Gather a 4 in circle of white rayon as shown, and fix to underside of hat, tucking fullness of raw edge round outer wire as padding. Gather similar circle of dress material and cover top. (d) Decorate top of hat with alternate bands of ruching (o) and gathered lace (m). Add bunch of flowers and long-tailed ribbon bow.

and broad ribbon ties at the front, under the chin (Figure 141 b).

If straw is unobtainable, make a hat of the dress material, and a toning deeper shade of the same colour, or white. Wire two circles, 3 in and 2 in in diameter, join them, and make a shallow crown as shown (Figure 142). Cover the crown with two 3 in circles of white cotton, gathered to fit, and the brim with rings of cotton, 4 in outer diameter and $1\frac{3}{4}$ in inside. Stitch the inner side of the ring to the crown cover, and turn the raw edges of the bottom ring over the wire, stitching firmly round it, then turn the raw edges of the upper ring to the under side, and hem into place. You now have a plain white hat, stiffened on a frame. Cover this, on the under side, with a 4 in circle of white rayon, gathered $\frac{1}{2}$ in, and 1 in from the raw edge, stitched into place, with the raw edge turned over to the upper side of the bonnet, and a line of retaining stitches at the crown edge. The top is covered with the dress material, in a 4 in circle, gathered in the same way. The raw edge is turned over to the underside, and hemmed very neatly into place, and the other edge of the gathers held by retaining stitches around the crown. Catch a few stitches through the crown also.

Trim the brim with a ruched frill of the same shade, then a lace or net frill, then the darker shade, then lace, and so on till the crown is covered. Add a bunch of feathers at the front, or flowers, sitting centrally in the first lace frill. Make a double ribbon bow, with long streamers, of the dress colour or the darker shade, and attach it at the centre back. Anchor the hat to the hair.

Also, make a parasol, by the same method, wiring a 5 in diameter wheel shape, with the spokes curved. Case all the spokes in doubled material or ribbon, in the deeper shade, then cover the frame with a 6 in diameter circle of dress material, with a $\frac{1}{4}$ in cut at the centre to let the ferrule through. Turn the raw edge over the outer wire, and hem down, then cover with the darker ribbon. Trim the outer edge, and round the ferrule, with fringing to match the dress fringe.

The parasol is mounted on a stick of round or turned wood, with a silver ferrule and handle, plus a cord or ribbon loop. The ferrule can have a tassel on a cord too. Hold the wooden handle in place with a wire from the cage, and stitching.

The 'secret pockets' in the skirt can contain a tiny lace hanky, tiny scissors, smelling salts, in a tiny gold phial, or any other miniature trinket.

Albert the Good (Plate 9)

Prince Albert worked hard and behaved well, which was a source of great irritation to some of the lazy, immoral politicians of his day. We show him in the uniform of the 11th Hussars (Prince Albert's Own), which he wore for the fatal Troop Review which led to his death of fever. Use a *Cloth Charles*, not thickened. *Albert* was a handsome man, with a moustache but no beard, and mid-brown hair receding from his forehead, with a small bald patch on top, and long, curly sideburns. There are many reproductions of Winterhalter portraits from which to make a head model (see Figure 26).

You may give *Albert* short drawers and a white shirt, though these will not show at all. His trousers are scarlet, and should look like wool. Cut them from Figure 78. When they are made up, add a broad gold ribbon stripe, down the outside of the leg, from waist to hem. The trousers would be worn over skin-tight, thin leather boots, but unless you can do these without making any ridge on the calf at all, it is simpler to make leather shoes, with square toes (Figures 39 a–c). Make a short strap of the trouser material, to go under the shoe at the instep, and hold the trousers tightly in position. He should also wear spurs, of which only the short gold bar with a revolving spiked wheel will show. A wire loop, with gold foil covered bar, and, if

Figure 143. Spur

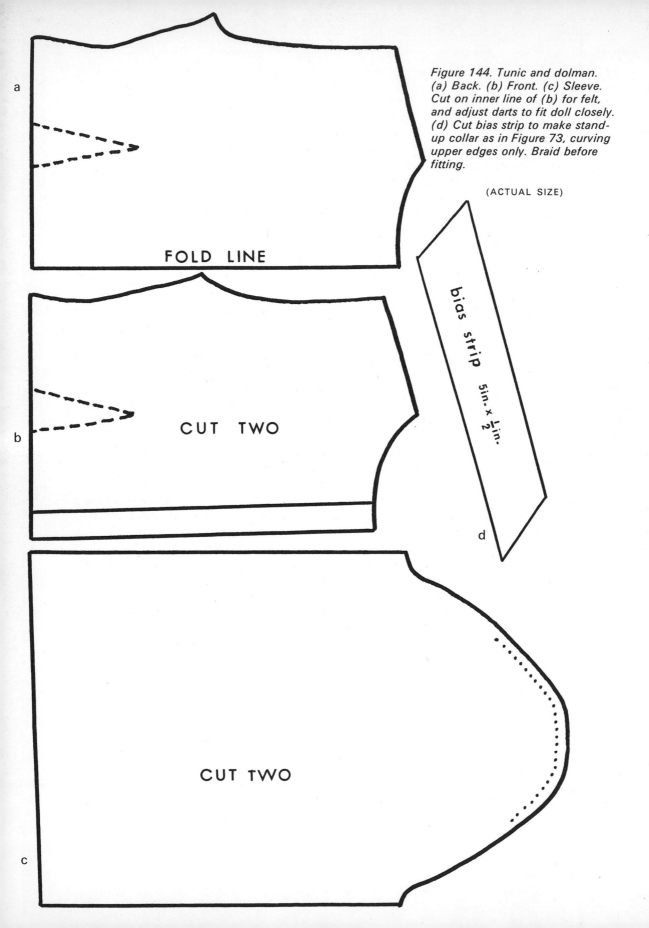

a

*Figure 144. Tunic and dolman.
(a) Back. (b) Front. (c) Sleeve.
Cut on inner line of (b) for felt,
and adjust darts to fit doll closely.
(d) Cut bias strip to make stand-
up collar as in Figure 73, curving
upper edges only. Braid before
fitting.*

(ACTUAL SIZE)

FOLD LINE

CUT TWO

b

bias strip 5in. x ½in.

d

CUT TWO

c

Victoria and Albert

Abraham and Mary Todd Lincoln

available, a toothed gear wheel from an old clock, will do very well (Figure 143).

Albert's tunic is cut in navy blue cloth — felt will be suitable here — and darted to fit like a second skin. Cut it as shown in Figures 144 a–d, dart, attach the tight sleeves, and the stand-up collar, but do not dress the figure yet. The whole front of the tunic has to be covered with horizontal bars of gold braid, from shoulder to shoulder at the top, tapering slightly towards the waist, but not to a point. Keep the bars on both fronts level, and stitch small gold buttons, real or embroidered, down each side and centre front. Braid completely round all edges of collar and wrist, doubling if necessary. (Figures 144 c and d). When braiding is complete, stitch on tunic, so the two sets of braid meet, but do not overlap.

Cut a dolman jacket, using the same patterns, lengthened by ½ in. Do not increase the width of the sleeves, because this style was never actually worn, but slung round the shoulders like a cloak. Edge the neck, on top of the collar band, the front edge and back, with brown fur, thicker at the neck than elsewhere. Gold braid the whole of the fronts, as for the tunic, broadly at the shoulder and tapering to the waist. Add a flourish in gold braid along the bottom hem, from the block of gold to the side seam (Figure 145).

Trim wrist with fur, and add a strip 1 in long up the arm, outlining wrist and strip in gold braid. The dolman is slung on the left

shoulder, with right side hanging loosely down the back, held by a plait of gold braid across the front of the chest. Albert also has a blue Garter ribbon, over his tunic, from the left shoulder downwards diagonally, and the sunburst badge with 'Honi Soit', etc. on his left breast. A loop of gold braid hangs from his right shoulder across to the centre of his chest.

This is his indoor wear, but he would add, for reviewing troops, white gloves, a sword and a busby. The gloves can be cut as simple palm shapes, with gauntlets, which are embroidered in gold thread, or outlined with paint. The sword is a cavalry sword, with a basket hilt minus wire cage, rather like *Charles II's*, but fatter (Figure 146). Decorate

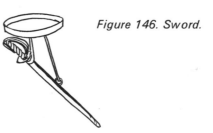

Figure 146. Sword.

the black scabbard with gold lines. The sword hangs from a leather belt across his left hip and a red ribbon sash, or is held in his right hand, like a walking stick.

The busby is a high pot-hat made in fur, which is held in position by a wire cage. Make two circles the size of *Albert's* head, and join them with uprights, finished length 2 in. If you are using real fur, cut a circle ½ in larger across, slitting the skin side, not cutting through the fur. Join to a strip 2½ in deep, and roughly 9 in long. Oversew the skins on the wrong side, and turn when seamed, then attach them to the wire frame at the bottom. If you are using fur fabric, increase the dimensions by ¼ in, for hemming, and take care not to get the pile twisted in the seam. The busby can be lined, with white cotton and dark rayon, if it is likely to be displayed off the head. It is decorated with a diagonal, gold-plaited cord, a white feather cockade, and a red silk 'bag' at the back (Figure 147). If he is displayed standing with *Victoria, Albert*

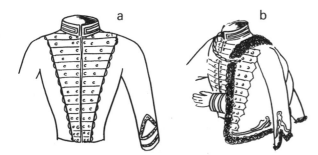

Figure 145. Braiding diagram.
(a) Tunic. (b) Dolman. Rows of gold buttons can be made of spirals of gold wire, or chain-stitched circles.

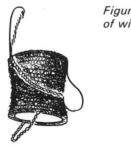

Figure 147. Busby, with detail of wire framework.

cloth bound round the neck like a bandage, and a cravat attached to it, made of three staggered layers of lace, which filled the front opening of his coat.

should carry his busby under his arm, fur forward. If he wears it, it is held on with a plaited gold strap, across the front of the chin.

George Washington (Plate 5)

George Washington wore the clothes of an English country gentleman of his day, adding epaulettes to denote his military status. Many portraits are available, including some on U.S. postage stamps, for designing a head, with the characteristic long nose and chin. His hair was a conventional powdered wig, like *Charles Edward's*, with three sausage side curls over each ear, and the other hair drawn back into a ribbon bow.

Give him drawers, if you wish, but very thin, so that they will not spoil the set of the tight breeches. These are cut from the pattern in Figures 82 a–b, made up, then slit on the outer side of the leg. Turn in the raw edge and lap the sides, so that the knee is grasped like a vice. Add four tiny buttons, and a little buckle at the bottom. The breeches are white, and can be either sateen or thin chamois or kid.

The high knee boots also fit like a skin, and can be cut in thin leather or sateen. Fit the leg on first, and then stitch the hard stuffed toe and sole section to it, outlining the heel with stitches. Add plain spurs, fitting over the ankle and around the heel. Use wire, or metal foil, and make the spur rowel from an old clock gear wheel, or from serrated foil (Figures 148 a–b).

George wore a white shirt, gathered at the neck (Figure 69), with plain muslin frilling on the sleeves. His neckwear was like *Charles Edward's*, a stock, of straight white

(ACTUAL SIZE)

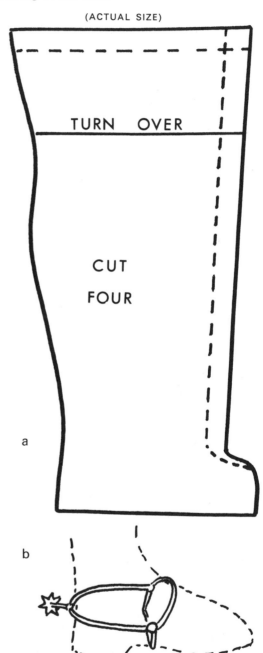

Figure 148. Boot leg pattern.
Use Figure 128 a–b for toe section, Adjust leg size to fit doll closely, allowing extra turnings if sateen is used. (b) Spurs.

His waistcoat or vest, again like *Charles Edward's*, was a light coloured brocade, cream, biscuit, very pale pastel, cut to the same pattern, though without any embroidery added. The buttons can be white, or toning with the cloth. Make the pocket flaps slightly smaller than for *Charles Edward*, and decorate them with cream or near same-coloured braid.

His coat is double-breasted, with deep, buttoned lapels, cut in one. They were worn open and buttoned back for official occasions, and casually buttoned across for home wear. Make it in blue cloth, darker than the sky-blue favoured in England, but not as dark as navy. Mid-blue felt or close-woven wool can be used, and the whole garment has a lining of red sateen. Cut both colours from the same patterns (Figures 149 a–d), and make up coat body and lining. The sleeves need not be fully lined. Attach collar and sleeves, turning in all raw edges and basting invisibly.

Make a row of 'buttonholes' down the front, on both sides, which can be simulated with strips of white tape, stitched neatly down on the red side, with a line down the middle of the tape to represent the 'hole'. If you wish to show the coat in 'campaign' position, turn back the lapels, and stitch them to the coat, with buttons fixed to every 'hole' (Figure 149 e). If you wish to show the domestic coat, then lap the projecting left front over the right, stitch two buttons over two holes on the blue side at stomach level, with the rest of the buttons down the fronts, $\frac{1}{2}$ in in from the edges (Figure 150). If you want to illustrate that the coat is versatile, then you will need to make real buttonholes down both fronts.

The cuffs are given holes all round the edge, with the buttons on the sleeve, at the point where the cuffs turn back to — or the buttons are stitched on top of the holes, when the cuffs are basted into position. The collar is faced in red, which shows since it is turned down, but not buttoned. *George* wears epaulettes, made of flat gold braid or ribbon tabs on his shoulders, with a thick fringe of gold wool hanging down (Figure 151). These

might be made from the thick cotton swags used for roping off displays at exhibitions. The coat has wide blue pocket flaps, lined with red, and bound with red, and buttons sewn on.

George has, for 'campaign' wear, a tricorn hat, white gloves and a sword. The gloves can be double or flat shapes in buckskin (simulated by kid or chamois) matching the breeches, and they are carried in the left hand, not worn. The sword is thin, with a narrow basket handle, no wire cage, but a large pommel (Figure 152). It can be made from wire, card and metal foil.

The three-cornered hat is of black felt, with a shallow crown, from a $3\frac{1}{2}$ in circle of felt slightly gathered, and a wide, stand-up brim. Cut this from a hollow circle of felt, $3\frac{1}{2}$ in internal diameter, and $1\frac{1}{2}$ in wide. Attach to the crown, oversewing with the brim sticking up, then make three even curls, with the fingers, in the outer edge. Stitch the brim to the crown between the curls, as in Figure 153, and add a huge rosette of red or blue ribbon to the edge of the brim. This is over the left eye, when worn. Trim the edge of the brim with red braid, matching that on the coat pockets.

Martha Washington (Plate 5)
The redoubtable *Mrs Washington* is made on a *Cloth Charlotte* doll, thickened in all dimensions, to suit her age. She also wears very much what an English lady of her social rank would have worn, with her hair powdered and dressed high, over pads, in a tower of curls. Make a longish crêpe hair wig, and pull all the hair backwards and upwards, in fat, sausage curls, except for the three side curls over the ears.

Martha can wear pantaloons, calf length, and/or a light cotton under-petticoat. Over this, she wears a hooped petticoat, like *Madame de Pompadour*, and her whole outfit is like *Madame's* without the frills and puffs. Make an over-petticoat of white cotton, edged with broderie anglaise, and an underskirt of light-coloured 'silk' — which can be

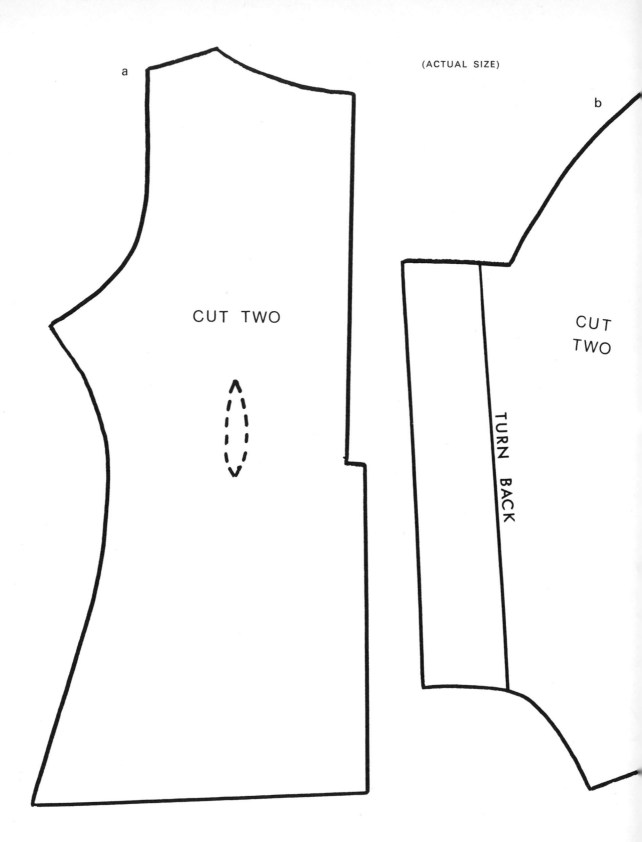

a

(ACTUAL SIZE)

b

CUT TWO

CUT
TWO

TURN BACK

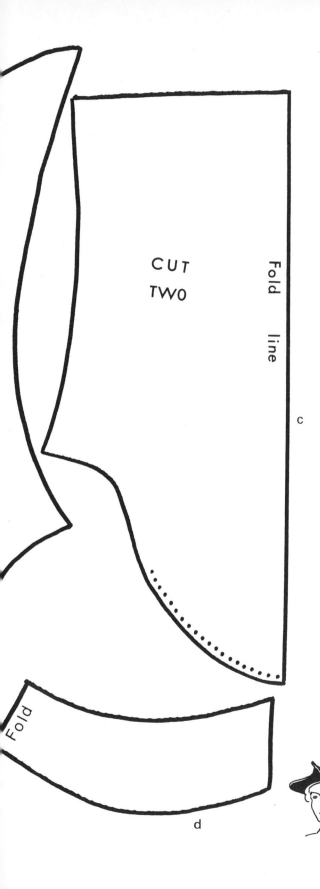

CUT

TWO

Fold line

c

Fold

d

Figure 149. Tail coat.
(a) Front. (b) Back. (c) Sleeve. (d) Collar.
Cut out all pieces in blue cloth and red lining.
Make up outer coat (a–c) leaving centre back
open below projection. Adjust darts to fit your
doll closely. Make up lining sleeves, and the
body of the coat in two halves. With right sides
facing, machine together the sleeves at the
cuff, and each side from the marked turning on
the neck to the centre back slit. Turn, and press
smooth. Finish armholes and shoulders by
hand. Lap one side of back slit under the other,
and turn in raw edges. The upper tail should
continue the centre back line. Make up collar,
and stitch as for Figure 70, with the red side
showing when turned back.

e

(e) Campaign position.
Turn back lapels on
marked line, stitch row of
taped button-holes down
both fronts with plain
buttons, real or simulated,
on top of each. Treat the
sleeve cuffs in the same way.

Figure 150. Domestic coat.
Tape button-holes down fronts
on the lining side. Add buttons
on top of tape for the upper
three on each lapel. Continue
row of buttons down blue face
of coat on the left side. Lap
left front over right and stitch
three buttons on edge of coat at
waist level. Complete the outer
row on the right-hand side.

Figure 151. Epaulettes.

Figure 152. Sword.

Figure 153. Tricorn hat.
Make up hat with brim pointing
upwards. Curl the edge between
the fingers, at front and sides, into
three sections. Tack to brim
between curls, and from side to
side of the curl if necessary. Braid
the upper edge and make ribbon
rosette for front.

taffeta or silky cotton — in lilac, pale mauve, pale green, ochre yellow, salmon pink, etc. This skirt is 9 in deep by 20 in wide, gathered to the waist, and edged at the bottom with frilling of the same colour. This is 1 in wide, with a pinked edge, and gathered tightly on the one edge, or 1½ in wide, with both sides turned in, and double gathered for ruching (see instructions for *Madame de Pompadour*).

Cut an overskirt, 9 in × 20 in, in the same material, and box-pleat the waist, to fit to within ½ in of the centre front. Make a line of gathers, half-way down the side of the skirt, to bunch up the material around the hips, but only a little (Figure 154). Frill or ruche in matching fabric all down the fronts of this skirt.

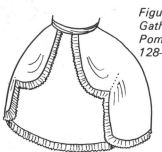

Figure 154. Martha's skirt. Gather and trim in modified Pompadour style (Figures 128–9).

Cut a close-fitting bodice, with a lowish, rounded front, in the same material (Figures 155 a and b). Since *Martha* was an old married lady, fill in the neck with a bib of fine pleated muslin, to the shape indicated (Figure 155d), cut from a strip of cloth and gathered. Her sleeves are edged with lace at the forearm and trimmed with ruching at the elbow.

Over her shoulders, she wears a triangular fichu, tucked in at the waist and crossing over at the front, lying loosely round the shoulders. This can be any light, semi-transparent fabric, from organdie edged with lace, or whole fine lace, to light sprigged muslin, in white or pastel. Around her waist, over the fichu, she has a sash of muslin or ribbon, in a deeper tone of the dress material, with hanging ends at the back (Figure 156).

She wears a huge mob-cap, made in white or figured organdie like the fichu, cut as a circle, 6 in diameter, and gathered and trim-

Figure 156. Mobcap and fichu in starched muslin, or figured lace.

med with 1 in wide frill of organdie or lace. Her hair is a white powdered wig, dressed high in a tower, like *Mme Pompadour's*, with a side ringlet. Trim the mob-cap with a ribbon bow to match dress or sash, with no tails. She should have a large fan, and a lace handkerchief. She may also carry a bunch of tiny keys, scissors, needle-case, etc. hanging from a gold chain at her waist. Her stockings are white, or dress coloured, and her shoes, styled like *Madame's*, match her dress or sash.

Mrs Amelia Bloomer (Cover)

Mrs Bloomer, inspired by the way men's clothes had been revolutionised by the introduction of trousers instead of breeches, tried to do the same for women's dress, and designed the first American women's trouser suit. Men and women alike recoiled in horror, and the crinoline, bustle and steel corset reigned supreme for many years to come.

Amelia is made on a *Cloth Charlotte* doll, with a small determined face, and fair hair parted in the middle bunched in tight ringlets at the side, hanging down. Make them by stitching to a tissue, and tearing it away later, as shown in Figure 24.

Her clothes have an Eastern or East European style. The famous bloomers are cut from the pantaloon pattern, doubled in width, and ankle length. They are in white or pastel cotton, and not at all transparent. Gather them tightly at the ankle and waist, completing the work on the doll. Over this, she

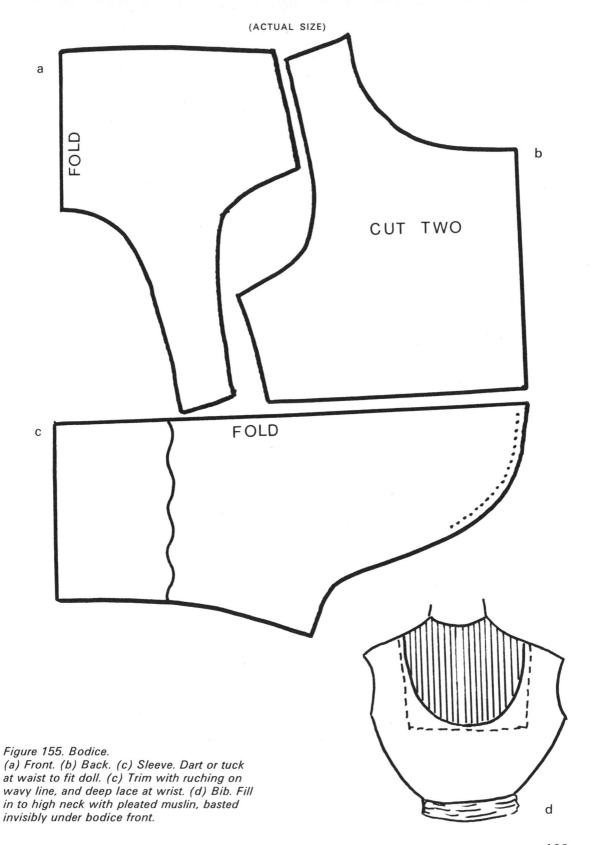

(ACTUAL SIZE)

a

FOLD

b

CUT TWO

c

FOLD

d

Figure 155. Bodice.
(a) Front. (b) Back. (c) Sleeve. Dart or tuck
at waist to fit doll. (c) Trim with ruching on
wavy line, and deep lace at wrist. (d) Bib. Fill
in to high neck with pleated muslin, basted
invisibly under bodice front.

wears a wide gathered skirt, wickedly short, to just below knee length. Cut in the same light fabric, and, if it does not stand out like a bell when gathered, add little pads of fabric at the hip, underneath. Keep most of the fullness at back and sides. Trim the hem with a band of floral embroidery, or patterned ribbon. The skirt should be about 5 in × 14 in, according to the fabric.

Her blouse is shirt-cut (Figures 69 a–c) and the high neck is gathered, also the wide sleeves, on to a narrow wrist band. Gather the neck, and trim with narrow lace. The material can be the same as the skirt, or fine white muslin.

Her jacket is of black nylon velvet, cut from Figures 157 a–c. The front is pointed, and the ends are basted down to the front skirt, like stomacher points. The front edges are trimmed with a band of floral embroidery on white, or with ribbon, to match the skirt. The sleeves are trumpet shaped, and forearm length, so that the chemise sleeves project from the ends. The jacket will sit better if it is lined, with white rayon. The front of the jacket closes together from just above the waist, and can have two or three little buttons on the floral band.

Her hat should be straw, made with a lowish crown with straight sides, and a wide brim. This brim is difficult to make in a small size, but if you do have straw that is flexible enough, build a crown, 1 in high, all the circumference of the head, and fill in the top with short lengths of straw, curved as far as possible, and stitched to fit the circle. Repeat with larger circles for the brim, stitching each row down flat on the next. You

Figure 158. Straw hat.
Bind all ragged edges of straw plait on brim. Plaited raffia is easier to handle. Trim with ribbon.

may manage to bend two-thirds of a circle, and fill in the rest at the back. The brim should be about 1 in wide. Trim with a ribbon with shoulder length streamers, which may be trained over the brim to conceal the joins (Figure 158). Otherwise cut a similar hat in white or cream felt, and trim with ribbon.

Her shoes are simple black slippers, as in Figure 159, worn over plain white stockings. In her hand, she might carry a rolled-up petition to Congress to rationalise women's dress, and in the other, a short riding whip, to beat off attacks from outraged papas, and neighbourhood dogs.

Figure 159. Slippers. Use pattern Figures 121 a–c, without heel piece.

Abraham Lincoln (Plate 10)

Lincoln's splendid craggy features are well known to everyone, and he can be modelled with or without a short beard, since he is familiar in both guises. His hair is rather short, but inclined to stick out in all directions, so do not make it stitched down closely at the back and sides. He was well over 6 ft tall, and thin in proportion, but by no means weak and weedy looking.

He had sombre tastes, and often wore all black, with only a white shirt to spice it. Occasionally, he wore a lighter waistcoat, or vest as it was by then described in America, but only pearl-gray, biscuit or beige, not a bright colour. Cut his suit in a close-woven wool, or wool-cotton mixture, and his vest in sateen or silky cotton. In life, he was a naturally untidy man, so creases in that vest would be appropriate.

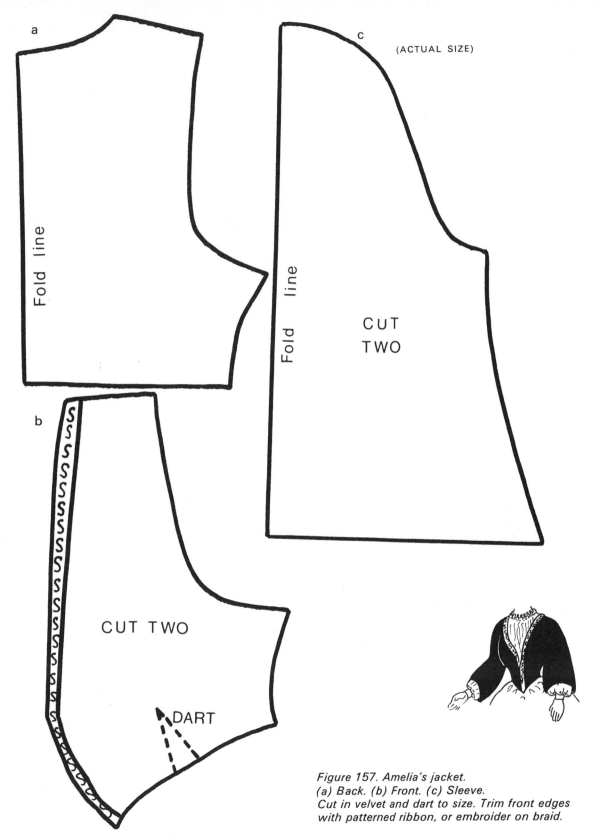

a

Fold line

c

(ACTUAL SIZE)

Fold line

CUT TWO

b

S S S S S S S S S S S S S S S S S S S

CUT TWO

DART

Figure 157. Amelia's jacket.
(a) Back. (b) Front. (c) Sleeve.
Cut in velvet and dart to size. Trim front edges
with patterned ribbon, or embroider on braid.

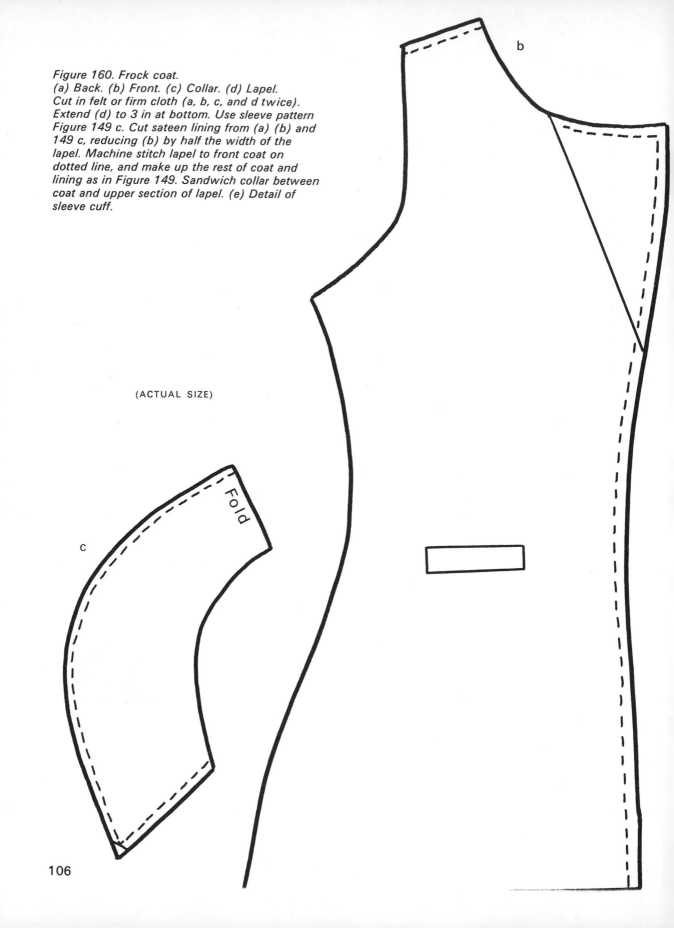

Figure 160. Frock coat.
(a) Back. (b) Front. (c) Collar. (d) Lapel.
Cut in felt or firm cloth (a, b, c, and d twice).
Extend (d) to 3 in at bottom. Use sleeve pattern
Figure 149 c. Cut sateen lining from (a) (b) and
149 c, reducing (b) by half the width of the
lapel. Machine stitch lapel to front coat on
dotted line, and make up the rest of coat and
lining as in Figure 149. Sandwich collar between
coat and upper section of lapel. (e) Detail of
sleeve cuff.

(ACTUAL SIZE)

b

c

Fold

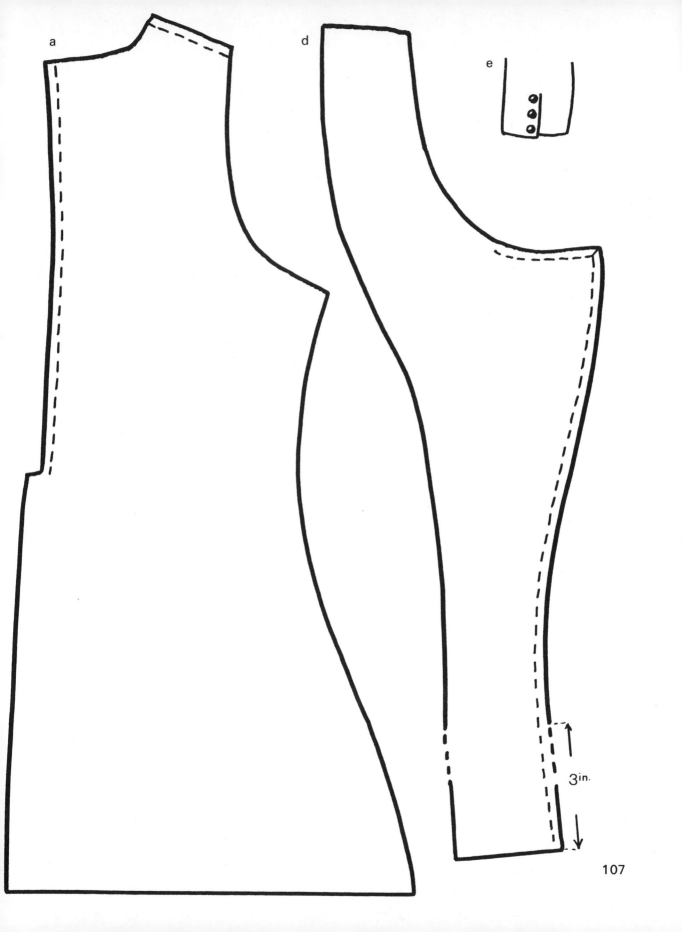

a

d

e

3in.

107

Cut a simple white shirt with a broad collar from Figures 69–70, gathering the sleeve end into a band. Turn over the collar rather high up the neck, and tie under it a broad band of black ribbon, tied in a wide, flat, rather untidy bow, with short ends. He would wear short drawers, of white or cream, and black wool trousers. Cut from the standard trouser pattern (Figure 78), and broadened by a $\frac{1}{4}$ in all round. Under these, give him black socks and black leather shoes cut to Figure 126.

His vest, black or a lighter colour, is single-breasted, cut to Figures 133 and 73 a, and can be lined. Lap the left side over the right very slightly, and stitch small black (or toning) buttons down the lower half.

His top coat is a black, broadcloth frock coat, knee-length, cut from Figures 160 a–d. Face it with the same material, if this is reasonably thin, or with black sateen, if the coat material would be too bulky. The lapels should lie neat and flat when turned back. Make, or simulate in black stitching, button-holes down the fronts, with black buttons close to them on the right front, and inside the left front. Line with black or very dark silky finish cotton or rayon, to make the coat hang properly. Add a pocket flap to each front where indicated. The bottom of the sleeve can either be slit for the last $\frac{1}{2}$ in, at the back, and then bound and stitched down, or it can be outlined in stitching, (see Figure 160 e). Three minute black buttons should be stitched on top of this slit, or indicated line. There is no practical purpose in the slit, but it was a design hangover from the turned back, buttoned cuff, as seen in *George Washington*.

Lincoln's accessories could be a law book, a handful of state papers or a quill pen, made of a feather.

Mary Lincoln (Plate 10)

Mrs Lincoln was a short, plump woman, with a broad face, full of character, and rather a worried look, from wondering what her husband would do next. She wore her hair parted in the middle, and drawn back round the ears like *Queen Victoria's*, with whom she had a lot in common.

Make long pantaloons, with lace at the ankles, a crinoline petticoat, like *Victoria's*, and a cotton over-petticoat, all 8 in deep, and in white. Her skirt is 9 in by 18 in, in a pale taffeta, and trimmed by four $\frac{3}{4}$ in flounces of the same material, at the bottom. The flounces should have embroidered or appliquéd floral motifs, and a band of ruched dress material along the top of the flounces.

The bodice is cut very low, and the sleeves are only short frills, so it may be as well to face the upper body and the arms with pink satin. If you are dissatisfied with the final effect, add a fine gauze or lace shawl over the costume. The bodice is basically a 1 in strip of straight material, fitted tightly round the body under the arms, and darted if necessary. Trim with two layers of wide frills, across bodice and shoulders, and three narrower frills round the arms, making the sleeves. Decorate the frills with floral motifs, like the skirt, and add a long swag of flowers, or fruit, and leaves, diagonally down the front of the dress, from bodice to hip level, as shown in Figure 161a. Artificial sprays of flowers can be bought, or made from green sateen with a pinked edge, for leaves, and ribbon rosebuds, with a wire linking stem, covered in green embroidery silk, as shown (Figure 161b).

In her hair, *Mary Lincoln* wears larger pink and white roses, mounted on a covered wire, in a crown shape, with short pink and white ribbon streamers. She wears white gloves, of kid or chamois, cut with the fingers in one piece, and marked with felt-tip pen. On her wrists, she wears silver bracelets, and a small necklace around her throat. In her right hand, she carries a handkerchief, of fine lace, and a large fan. In her left, as a macabre touch, she might have a theatre programme, for the performance of 'Our American Cousin', at which Lincoln was assassinated in 1865. She will wear white stockings and small black shoes, but these will be hidden under her dress.

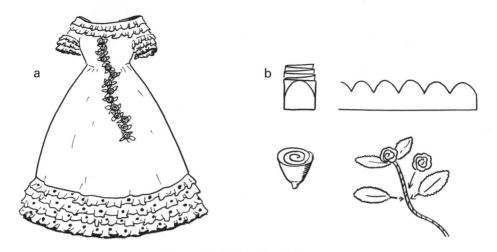

Figure 161. Mrs Lincoln's dress.
(a) General view (b) Roses. Cut strips of stiffened muslin, folded 4–6 times, into petal shape. Open out, roll into cylinder and secure bottom. Attach roses and muslin or plastic leaves to wire bound with green thread, and drape across skirt.

CHAPTER 9

Little People

Dolls for individual display are usually a foot high, or even larger, for convenience in working, and for showing detail adequately. However, smaller dolls are required for most dolls' houses, and for group work, in making scenes which include landscape features and often several figures.

Dolls' house dolls should be designed with the recipient in mind. Some small children appreciate minute detail, and will care for replicas into which a great deal of work has gone. For them, it is worth using the expertise gained on making larger dolls, and scaling everything down to the smaller size. Some children are natural born destroying angels, and for them wooden peg dolls, or the cheapest bought toys, are good enough, dressed with a cheap, cheerful, hint at a national or period style only, if you wish.

Group models, as made by families, school classes, or women's clubs, are a different proposition. They are usually static, not handled every five minutes, mostly fixed to a base, and sometimes not subject to close scrutiny. Occasionally, too, they have to be made quickly, and are not meant to last long, so that elaborate detail is out of the question. The important thing is the impression they give at first sight, not the subtle beauties under the fourth layer of clothes.

The fundamental differences between large and small doll work are shared — the smaller amount of stiffening needed, the greater simplicity of the trimming, and a different method of cutting out and making up the garments. It is even more necessary to avoid hems, and work in fabrics, like felt, which need none, or can be pinked or flat basted,

without risk of fraying. For short-lived models, it is worth using the right fabric, and trusting it not to fray before next week. Spray starch will sometimes fix an edge, and colourless glue is invaluable. The important thing is to achieve the desired impression, even if some of the details are absent.

A useful framework doll can be made from corks and wire, which will serve most group modelling purposes. The kind of corks most generally useful are the short fat corks used in many wine bottles, which have a round plastic top crimped on to them. This is easily prised off, and can be used as a base for the figure. Pick smooth corks for faces, and use any pitted corks for bodies. Join three corks by a wire, as shown, to make the head and body. Add two wires for legs, and two shorter ones for arms (Figure 162). Normally, loop the ends of the arms, but leave the legs as spikes, which can then be stuck into the base board.

Wire alone, wound into a body with projecting limbs, and given a small ball head, (Figure 163) will serve for some purposes, but the lack of bulk is awkward. If you are making a model where the aim is

Figure 162. Cork and wire framework doll. Use smooth cork for head.

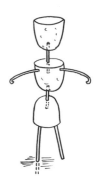

a

b

Figure 163. Wire doll with polystyrene (Styrofoam) ball head. (b) Pad arm or body with cotton wool, held in place by stockinet strip, stitched firmly at ends. Hands may be padded if nothing is to be carried.

lightness, and even weightlessness, then single wire, or white pipe-cleaners may do. See, for example, the *Ballerina* (Figure 164). She is dressed in very thin organdie, gathered round her in two layers, to stand out like a tutu, topped with two white birds' feathers, a white ball head, and painted hair. She looks as if a puff of wind would blow her away — which is fine for ballerinas, or fairies at the bottom of the garden, but not strong enough for soldiers, shepherds, kings, etc. Non-action figures can be made of plastic bottles, with ball heads, and arms of stiffened fabric, provided that their lower limbs are covered.

Keep the heads simple: balls, ovals, even flat discs with no moulded features, and the minimum painted detail. Make the clothes from oblongs, strips, squares, circles, as far as possible. Subtle curves do not show, and make fitting awkward. Most of the joining and shaping is done on the body, but hems and trimmings have to be completed first, if they require access to both sides of the cloth. Run gathering thread loosely, and pull tight after fitting on the body.

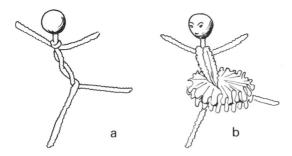
a   b

Figure 164. Ballerina.
(a) Pipe-cleaner and ball head framework.
(b) Gathered muslin tutu and feather bodice.

The Holy Family

A project which is frequently undertaken at Christmastime is a crib scene, to be displayed on a table. The scene will include an open stable, with real straw, if possible, cattle stalls, animals, a manger and surrounding hills. The figures are *Mary, Joseph* and *The Baby, Three Kings,* and *Three Shepherds.*

THE BABY is a tiny swaddled figure — just a ball head and white bandages, but set him on a mirror, to reflect a light source from above, to shine on himself and his mother. This is safer than a bulb hidden among straw.

MARY is the central figure, and must shine even against the brightness of the *Three Kings.* Dress her all in one colour — a rich, heavenly blue is traditional, get her in a spotlight, and leave a space round her. Absolutely no one else in the whole scene should wear blue or turquoise.

Make a 4 in high cork and wire framework doll, as above, choosing a very smooth cork for the face, which is painted pale pink all over, then given eyes and a mouth, but no nose. Curve the head top with a small piece of stuck-on cork, or pad with kapok, under a small muslin frill in white, which will be seen at the front of the headdress.

Cut a strip slightly longer than neck to waist, and an inch longer than the circumference of the 'chest' cork (about $1\frac{1}{2}$ in by $4\frac{1}{2}$–5 in, for a 4 in doll). Bind this round as a bodice, gathering the neck to fit, and making a small slit for one arm wire. Pad the arm loop with either kapok and stockinet, or a scrap of felt, to make a hand, since this shows, and cut a cylindrical wide sleeve (about 1 in by $1\frac{1}{2}$ in) gathered loosely at both ends, and pulled tight when fitted to the doll. Cut a wide skirt, about $2\frac{1}{2}$ in deep by 8 in wide, gathered at the top. Seat the doll, and spread the skirt well out round her legs, which can be spiked in the base to steady her. If she is set on a stool, made of a cork with its plastic top intact, this can be stuck or spiked to the base as well. Cut a circle of the blue material,

9 in in diameter, fold it in half, and fix the centre to the top of her head. Train the doubled folds down each side, and spread out the curve of the cloak around the seated figure, catching it down on either side of the face, to form a close hood.

Set one hand on the manger, and the other pointing out, forwards. A halo is traditional, but looks clumsy if wired to the head with a circle. Make one in silver wire or foil and aim to suspend it from a very fine thread above her, or on a wire spike attached to the manger or stable, behind her.

JOSEPH has a browner face, and a thin gray beard stuck to his lower jaw, made in crêpe hair, gray wool or dyed string. He wears an indoor cap, like a loose turban. Attach a head-shaped pad of cotton wool to a 1 in square of white or pale cream cloth, fix on top of the head, and loosely wind the rest of the strip twice around the head. You will need about 1 in by 9 in (Figure 165).

Figure 165. Holy Family.
Place Baby on mirror or silver foil, to reflect concealed light above. Seat Mary on wood block or extra cork, and use leg wires to hold out skirt. Joseph stands in background, with hands linked in gesture of welcome.

Make him a white gown, of two oblongs of cloth, about 3 in by 2 in, joined at sides and shoulders. Make white sleeves, wide and loose at the wrist, to cover his hands.

His robe can be striped in dull red or any dark shade, or gray, or off-white, as long as he avoids brown, yellow, ochre, sand, etc, which you will need for the *Shepherds*,

and red, purple or other bright colours you will use for the *Kings*. Washed-out pyjama stripes, or ticking will fill the bill. Cut one T-shaped piece, and two L shaped pieces, to the dimensions shown in Figure 166, and join at sides and shoulders. Stand *Joseph* to the back of the scene, behind *Mary* and the *Baby* at one side, with his hands clasped together on his stomach, and his elbows out, in gesture of welcome. Spike his legs to the base.

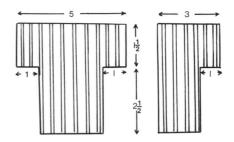

Figure 166. Robe pattern for 4 in doll (basic). *May be worn open over a sleeveless gown, or closed across front.*

THE SHEPHERDS all have striped cloaks, and striped or deep buff gowns, on the same design as *Joseph's*. If possible, go for variety, and have non-matching stripes, but all should have brown, sand, ochre, yellow, dull orange, etc. in them, as protective colouring in the desert. One's gown can match another's cloak, of course. Their headdresses are white, or cream, cloths, 5 in square, draped over a cotton wool pad, and left hanging down the back of the neck. They are held around the head by a band of plaited wool, tied round twice and knotted (Figure 167).

Figure 167. Shepherd.
Vary colours of gowns and robes, in brown or dull yellow shades. Secure head-cloth with plaited coloured wool ring.

Make the *Three Shepherds*, and give them wooden twigs as staffs, with a natural crook in the end if possible. One might carry a lamb, made of pipe-cleaners twisted round cotton wool (Figure 168). Station them at the front to the left of *The Holy Family*, not obscuring the manger scene.

Figure 168. Lamb.
Scale down Figure 98, or use two small pieces of cotton wool for body and head, winding pipe cleaner round to keep them in place. Hook separate short lengths for legs through body wire.

THE THREE KINGS are traditionally, and reasonably, Eastern, one being often shown as Ethiopian. Dress them in bright robes, with any shade of red, green, bright yellow or bright orange, but avoiding blue or turquoise. Trim with scraps of gold braid, or other bright, tinselly ribbon, of which quite small pieces will go a long way.

Caspar wears a patterned broad robe, cut from the cloak pattern, reversed for fitting on, that is, with the opening down the back, to be stitched together later. The robe might be red, orange, bright pink, with a stylised, preferably circular pattern in black or a bright colour. Trim with darkish braid, with a (Lurex) metal thread, at bottom, neck and sleeve edges. He carries a long gold staff with a knob. Use black crêpe or string, in short tight sausage curls for the beard, and shoulder-length frizzy ringlets for the hair (Figure 169). He wears a circular gold crown, in serrated edged gold foil, on his head (Figure 170). He will need stockinet arms over his wire.

Figure 169. Caspar.

Figure 170. Crown, in card or foil.

Melchior wears a light, but not pastel, mauve or apple-green robe, cut like *Joseph's* gown, and gold-braided around the bottom. Make him stockinet covered arms, in pale brown and trim the top with a scrap of the gold braid, as a sleeve. Make him a straight cloak, from a strip of purple cloth, 3 in wide, which is gathered at one end, attached to the left shoulder, and wrapped loosely round, under the right arm, across the front, gathered on the left shoulder again and anchored with a gold clasp (button), and then left to hang down the back. (Figure 171).

Figure 171. Melchior's cloak. Attach gathered end to top of left shoulder, and drape round, loosely, sewing clasp to the cloak where it meets the shoulder again.

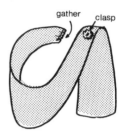

His beard is in the same vertical sausage curls, but longer, whereas his hair is in looser curls (Figure 172). His hat is a 'mitre' cap, cut in purple felt to fit the head at the bottom, and half as big at the top. Cut as Figure 173 and join along the bulge at the front, covering the join with a triangle of green felt. Give him a gold foil bracelet or two on his arms. He carries a short gold rod, with either a crook or a knob at the end.

Figure 172. Melchior.

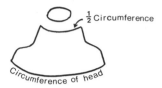

½ Circumference

Circumference of head

Figure 173. Melchior's mitre.
Cut in felt, to fit cork head at bottom. Cross stitch together up front of hat and cover the stitching with a green triangle of felt, pointing upwards.

Balthasar is very dark, wears a short pointed beard, and what can be seen of an 'Afro' hair style under his large white turban. Make this of a folded 2 in strip of muslin or rayon, twisted round three times over a pad of cotton wool, till it sits up well, and 'fastened' with a red jewel.

He wears red or bright yellow trousers, very wide, cut as gathered cylinders, 2 in deep, and stitched to the lower body. On top, he has a bright short gown, cut from two squares, 2 in by 2 in, joined at sides and shoulders. Trim the bottom edge and down one side with contrasting ribbon, preferably with a metallic thread. Give him cylindrical sleeves in the trousers colour, and gather them at both ends. Also make a 2 in deep cloak, in dark red, deep green etc., gathered at the neck, and attached to the shoulders (Figure 174).

All the figures with long gowns, who are standing upright, could be made from plastic bottles, which would replace the body and legs. The arms could be made of wires spiked into the top of the bottle, or as stiffened sleeves, sewn into the side of the robes. If some kind of weight is put in the bottom of the bottles, they will stand by themselves. In any case, the broader bases give a better area for sticking (Figure 175).

On the same principle, very small skittles, with rounded head and cylindrical body, will convert into small dolls. Scrub the paint off, and redecorate the 'face'. Any short fat piece of wood, topped by a ball can be used. Polystyrene (Styrofoam) balls in many sizes are obtainable, which paint up nicely as faces (Figure 176).

Figure 174. Balthasar.
Detail of turban. Pad the head and anchor end of cloth to pad in centre, loose end pointing back. Wind round back, front and over back, below first twist. Complete by crossing from doll's left eye, upwards diagonally to right, and round back, tucking loose end inside turban. Stitch down and jewel top.

Figure 175. Male and Female shampoo bottle dolls with ball heads, for use with full length robes. Add stones as ballast.

Skittle

Wire loop

Roll of card

Figure 176. Two methods of stiffening arms. Make up robe and insert wire loop, with padding for bulk, or roll of card. Stitch end of sleeve across, to hold stiffener.

114

CHAPTER 10

Mounts

Well-made costume dolls are works of art, worth displaying when complete. If they are put away in a box together, they get crumpled, and scratchy bits of one doll's costume get hooked on other dolls, and damage them. They can be wrapped singly, tucked in individual shoe boxes, and bolstered round with tissue paper, but every time anyone wants to see, they may get pulled out awkwardly, and spoiled. Ideally, they should be kept where they can always be seen, displayed so that all of them can be seen without too much handling. A purpose-built cabinet, lined with mirrors to show the back details, with glass doors, is perhaps a dream, but small book shelves, with a closed back, can be adapted by sticking on mirror tiles, or pretty wall-paper as backgrounds. A transparent plastic cover can be pinned over this when any dusty operations are taking place, to cut down the amount of handling needed for cleaning.

To hold the dolls steady in their positions, some form of mount is necessary, since a dressed doll has no leg muscles to balance herself with, and tends to tip over. Here are some ways to mount your dolls. (Figure 177).

(a) is suitable for small dolls fixed in a landscape, spiked directly to the base.

(b) and (c) are spiked, by the leg wires or a wire from the base, to a wooden disc or block. They can be handled by the base. Suitable for dolls with not too much weight at the top.

(d) and (e) For dolls heavy at the top, a spike from a wooden base into the mid section. (e) is seated on a thread spool. Spikes are concealed under skirts.

(f) For male figures, a spike into the back from the rear of the display shelf for top heavy figures.

All spikes are liable to damage the area they fix into, and the following mounts are less injurious.

(g) An elastic loop round the waist of the doll holds it firmly, but the doll is not easy to detach, and the back skirt may crumple.

(h) and (i) Rigid wire cages, placed under the skirt at waist height, allow the doll to be lifted out easily. Unsuitable for male figures.

(j) A wooden base with a wire upright and loop well above the head with thin threads holding neck and waist, for male figure, not too heavy.

(k) Wooden base with upright, and wired arms at waist and neck, curved around the figure closely enough to hold any figure steady.

(l) The de-luxe version of this, with upright bound with ribbon, and arms padded with cotton wool, etc., and covered with strip of silky material (m), gathered along its length, and lace trimmed if desired. If this matches the dressed doll, it will be attractive, and not obtrusive. One padded wire at waist level will probably be enough to support the doll.

Wooden bases should be painted, either black or matching the base of your display cabinet. If a particular doll would need a large base to balance its weight, which would take up too much room in the cabinet, try sticking or screwing a metal disc under the wood, to add weight without size. Alternatively, cut recesses in the base of the shelf, to take the wooden base. As an extra precaution for a really weighty doll,

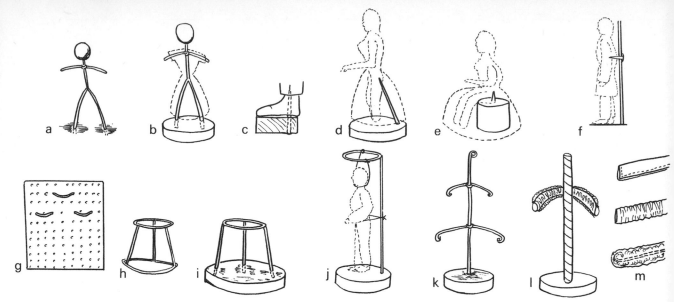

Figure 177. (a)–(m) Mounts for displaying dolls.

anchor the base in its recess with a small turn-buckle fastener. The better the doll has been made, with a strong wire framework and rigid stuffing, the better it will balance with the slightest assistance from its mount.

If you are asked to provide a single doll, or pair of dolls, for a display of craft work, then it is worth making an individual frame for it or them. This can be as simple as an illustration of the landscape of the country, for a national doll, a rich silk or velvet drape hanging behind a historical doll, or if time permits, a more complicated 'set' in a box framework, with a wallpaper or tapestry background, of upholstery material, can be made. The sides of the box represent the walls of the room, and items of the right period in history can be added to create the right atmosphere. Often, magazine articles on art and antiques will provide illustrations of old paintings, mirrors or even three-dimensional looking furniture. Cut these out carefully, and stick direct to the wall fabric, or in the case of furniture, on a piece of cardboard or block of polystyrene, fixed to the wall.

Actual models of furniture, in balsa wood, cardboard or papier mâché, can be used, and 'period' mirrors can be made very effectively from toy or vanity mirrors, with a stuck-on frame of metal foil, paper doily or coarse lace, dyed gold, silver or black. Don't get too carried away, though. An appropriate background and one, or two pieces of wall decoration or furniture looks fine. A whole mass of bits and pieces in the foreground distracts attention from the doll, which is the chief exhibit.

The box framework can be a shoe-box, or a small wooden affair, which doubles as a carrying case to take the doll to the exhibition. Pack it round with balls and strips of tissue paper to limit movement. Add a neatly lettered label with the name or description of the doll — embossed letters on black plastic tape look well, or black drawing ink on white card. If the exhibition lasts longer than an afternoon, and you will not be there to keep an eye on the doll, it is as well to add, on the back of the box, your name and address to ensure safe return. Also, if any of the 'produce' at the show might be sold in aid of charity, and your doll is only on loan, write on the box "Not for Sale", or you may be faced with tracing, and trying to recover, the model you need for another display the week after, from a tearful infant whose Grandmama bought it for a few pence from a junior helper. Costume dolls are always popular sellers for charitable causes, so, if you have time, and could make a few dolls for sale, or a special one to raffle, the organisation would profit by your efforts, and everyone would be happy.

APPENDIX

Some Useful Costume Books

History of Costume

Cassin-Scott, Jack, *Fashion and Costume in Color: 1760–1920*, The Macmillan Co., New York, N.Y., 1972.

Hansen, Henry H., *Costumes and Styles: The Evolution of Fashion from Early Egypt to the Present*, E. P. Dutton & Co., Inc., New York, N.Y., 1972.

Laver, James, *Costume Through the Ages*, Simon & Schuster, Inc., New York, N.Y., 1964.

Lister, Margot, *Costumes: An Illustrated Survey from Ancient Times to the Twentieth Century*, Herbert Jenkins, London, Plays, Inc., Boston, Mass., 1968.

Payne, Blanche, *History of Costume*, Harper & Row, Publishers, New York, N.Y., 1965.

Stavridi, Margaret, *History of Costume* (4 volumes), Plays, Inc., Boston, Mass., 1966–1970.

Waugh, Norah, *The Cut of Women's Clothes*, Theatre Arts Books, New York, N.Y., 1968.

Wilcox, R. Turner, *Dictionary of Costume*, Charles Scribner's Sons, New York, N.Y., 1969.

American Costume

Earle, Alice M., *Two Centuries of Costume in America* (2 volumes), Dover Publications, Inc., New York, N.Y., 1970.

Gorsline, Douglas, *What People Wore*, The Viking Press, Inc., New York, N.Y., 1952.

McClellan, Elizabeth, *History of American Costume*, Tudor Publishing Co., New York, N.Y., 1969.

Wilcox, R. Turner, *Five Centuries of American Costume*, Adam and Charles Black, London, Charles Scribner's Sons, New York, N.Y., 1963.

British Costume

Bradfield, Nancy, *Historical Costumes of England*, Barnes & Noble, Inc., New York, N.Y., 1971.

Brooke, Iris, *English Costume* (a series of 6), Methuen, London, Barnes & Noble, Inc., New York, N.Y., 1963–1964.

Calthrop, Dion Clayton, *English Costume 1066–1830* (4 volumes), Adam and Charles Black, London, 1950, Macmillan, New York & Toronto.

Cunnington, C. Willett & Phillis, *Handbook of English Costume* (a series of 5), Faber and Faber, London, Plays, Inc., Boston, Mass., 1969–1973.

Cunnington, Phillis & Mansfield, Alan, *English Costume for Sports & Outdoor Recreation*, Barnes & Noble, Inc., New York, N.Y., 1970.

Fox, Lilla M., *Costumes and Customs of the British Isles*, Plays, Inc., Boston, Mass., 1974.

European Costume

Fairservis, Walter A., *Costumes of the East*, Chatham Press, Riverside, Conn., 1971.

Fox, Lilla M., *Folk Costumes of Southern Europe*, Plays, Inc., Boston, Mass., 1972.

——, *Folk Costumes of Western Europe*, Plays, Inc., Boston, Mass., 1971.

Kretschmer, Albert, *Die Trachten der Völker*, Leipzig.

Mann, Kathleen, *Peasant Costume in Europe*, Adam and Charles Black, London, Humanities Press, Inc., New York, N.Y., 1950.

Index